2

8534

SOLOMON'S
CHILDREN

SOLOMON'S CHILDREN

Exploding the Myths of Divorce

Glynnis Walker

Arbor House / New York

Manufactured in the United States of America

10 9 8 7 6 5 4 3 2 1

Library of Congress Cataloging in Publication Data

Walker, Glynnis, 1951–
    Solomon's children.

    Bibliography: p. 215
    1. Divorce—United States.   2. Children of divorced parents—United States—Attitudes.   3. Custody—United States.   I. Title.
HQ834.W34   1986   306.8′9   85-19958
ISBN: 0-87795-748-7

Design by Laura Hough

To my Mother and my Grandmothers,
women who have always
stood on their own two feet
_____

Acknowledgments

My sincere appreciation to all those who took the time to fill out the questionnaire. Though it may have been difficult for some of you to relive the experience of your parents' divorce, your willingness to confront your feelings and your unique perspective will help prevent others from becoming Solomon's Children.

Contents

Chapter One: Solomon's Decision   *1*

What Adults Don't Know   *2*   •   "We Are Not
Your Pawns"   *3*   •   Conflicting Research   *5*
  •   Parental Wish-Perception   *8*   •   The Di-
vorce Industry   *10*   •   Facing the Facts   *11*

Chapter Two: The Children of Light   *13*

The Questionnaire   *15*   •   Who Answered the
Questionnaire?   *27*   •   "It's Time Someone
Heard Our Side"   *30*

Chapter Three: The Rise of the Child-King   *34*

The Child in Recent History *36* · Children
as a Resource *40* · The Child as a Consumer *44* · The Child as a Political
Force *46* · "For the Sake of the Children" *47*

Chapter Four: The Motherhood Myth   *50*

Mothers and Divorce *51* · Maternalism, the
State, and Society *54* · Maternalism and
Power *57* · Momism, U.S.A. *59* · Exam-
ining the Instinct Issue *62* · With Quiet
Consent *65* · The Other Side of the
Myth *70*

Chapter Five: The Daddy Dilemma   *71*

Mommy "Mavins" and Daddy "Bank-
ers" *73* · The "Delinquent Daddy" and the
"Deserted Child" *75* · The Custody
Wars *82* · The Custody Configura-
tion *86* · The Custody Conclu-
sion *88* · Why Fathers Are So
Important *90*

Chapter Six: The Divorce Equation   *93*

Why Work Is a Four-Letter Word *95* · Why
Women Don't Work *97* · "Daddy, I Need
My Check" *101* · The Uniform Marriage
and Divorce Act *103* · The Hidden Costs of
Child Support *104* · What Divorce Denies
the Children *107* · Varying Support

Orders   *108*   ·   The Trust Alternative   *112*   ·   Forcing the Support Situation   *114*   ·   Stepparent Support   *117*   ·   No
More Daddy Deductions   *118*

Chapter Seven: How Children Feel About Divorce   *120*

Finding Out How Children Feel   *120*   ·   Chil-
dren's True Feelings About Divorce   *122*   ·
Frequently Expressed Feelings   *126*   ·
A Case of Parental Seduction?   *133*   ·
Guilty as Charged?   *134*   ·
One More Time?   *134*   ·
Feelings in the Long Term   *136*   ·
How the Feelings of Adults Fit in   *139*   ·
Divorce—a Rite of Passage?   *141*

Chapter Eight: The Future Family   *142*

The Serial Marriage   *145*   ·   Taking
Steps   *147*   ·   Other People's Children   *149*   ·   Other People's People   *151*   ·   Steps as
Parents   *155*   ·   Stepfamily Pluses and Minuses   *159*   ·   You Don't *Have* to Love Each
Other   *162*

Chapter Nine: Custody and Common Sense   *165*

Custody and the Law   *167*   ·   Creating a
"Power Parent"   *170*   ·   The Plight of Mothers
Who Don't Want Custody   *170*   ·   Could You
Be a Custody Criminal?   *171*   ·   Federal Par-
ent Locator Service   *175*   ·   Being in Con-
tempt   *175*   ·   Custody
Arrangements   *176*   ·

States with Joint Custody *178* · The Pros
and Cons of Joint Custody *180* · Profile of a
Joint Custody Parent *183* · How to Go
About Joint Custody *184* · The Joint Custody Agreement *185*

Chapter Ten: Divorce—A New Beginning   *188*

Divorce in the Long Term *189* · The Chil-
dren of Wisdom *192* · Can Divorce Be
Catching? *197* · How the Children Would
Do It Better *200* · The Truth About the
Consequences *207*

References   *215*

SOLOMON'S
CHILDREN

Chapter One

Solomon's Decision

Then Solomon said, "Bring me a sword." So they brought a sword for the king. He gave then an order: "Cut the living child in two and give half to one and half to the other."

The woman whose son was alive was filled with compassion for the child, "Please, my lord, give her the living baby! Don't kill him!"

But the other woman said, "Neither I nor you shall have him. Cut the child in two!"

I Kings 3:24–26

Over 1 million American children were involved in their parents' divorce last year, and we are doing many of these children a great disservice. We treat them like damaged goods or, worse, we bend over backward to "make it up to them somehow." We pity them. We think they are different, and we make them think they are different.

Divorce is no longer a rarely used solution to the problem of an unhappy marriage: Half of the over 2 million couples who get married in the United States this year will end up getting divorced. On average, one child will be involved in each of those divorces. It is time that we took another look at how we perceive these "children of divorce."

In spite of what many people prefer to believe (whether for social, religious, or personal reasons), the "children of divorce" are not always condemned to be the emotionally and psychologically broken beings we have incorporated into our divorce mythology. They can be resilient. They can adjust well to their parents' divorce, if we would only let them. Often they cope with divorce a lot better than the adults around them.

This book is written in the hope that it will release the children of divorce from many of the misconceptions that surround their lives. It will reveal that it is our outdated notions abut the ending of a marriage, plus our desire to serve our own needs, that is currently clouding our perception of how children react to divorce. It is time to give the children of divorce, no matter what their age, a chance to tell how they really feel and to examine our currently faulty approach to divorce in light of their perceptions.

WHAT ADULTS DON'T KNOW

When I began the research for this book, I had only one preconceived idea, and that was this: When it comes to divorce, the adults don't really know what the children are thinking. Because of this breakdown in communication a lot of people are blaming themselves for the pain and suffering in their children's lives, when in fact their children are sighing with relief that their parents finally "did it." Also, having examined the divorce process in other research and discussed it individually with hundreds of people—men, women, and children—in several countries, I realized that the whole business of divorce and its aftermath is becoming more and more cockeyed. Rather than improving the condition of the "children of divorce," we are making things decidedly worse. Many of the problems that can erupt for the children after a divorce are brought about directly by the system that is supposed to prevent them.

I wanted to give the people who had been through their parents' divorce the chance to really tell, in their own words, how they felt about their experience, what they thought was wrong (and right) with the way it was handled, and how the divorce of their parents affected their own marriages and later lives.

I was not prepared for some of the results I got. For instance, living in a society where Mom, America, and Apple Pie is the cultural trilogy of an era, I was surprised that so many children of divorce were more than ready to move Mom out of the trilogy and replace her with Dad. What was most interesting about this particular response was how widely it was shared: Older and younger people expressed it, as did people of many different financial, educational, and cultural backgrounds. This indicates strongly that the divorce process and, perhaps, our perceptions of family life have been at odds with reality for too long.

"WE ARE NOT YOUR PAWNS"

Perhaps change is on the way. People are beginning to see the situation for what it is, and it is not just those who were concerned enough to answer my questions, but other people, too, across the country.

The following letter appeared in a newsletter called *Justice* that is published by the Fathers for Equal Rights of America, a nonprofit men's rights group in Michigan:

> I am a child of divorce. My parents' divorce became finalized in 1969 when I was six years old. My mother was granted custody and my father never fought it.
> I wish to see change. Change in a system that

helped to alter my relationship with my father for the duration of our lives. My father began his weekend visits, but in his absence he had become a stranger, a curiosity to me. And, a new set of rules was imposed on our house. My father was spoken of very little. I only heard his name as he was being chastised for not visiting or blamed for a check that never arrived or came later. From 8 to 18 I was a very cynical, negative, aggressive individual. Today when I see my father we follow a pattern of behavior dictated by those lost moments.

I am only articulating what children caught in today's divorce process are experiencing and cannot voice themselves. We are not your pawns.

The following letter was sent to me by a nineteen-year-old girl whose parents divorced when she was seven:

I filled out the questionnaire because I have often wanted the chance to explain to "the world" that I'm not a social misfit just because my parents are divorced. People are constantly offering such patronizing remarks as, "Poor dear. She comes from a broken home you know" or, "She has trouble at school because she has only one parent at home."

The situation with my parents is ideal. In certain aspects I feel much better off by having just one parent. I learned to become more independent as did my sisters. I also feel it was the divorce that brought my sisters and me closer together. I don't know anyone else who is as close to their family as I am. From my point of view divorce is not so terrible. I do not think that the divorce caused a disruption in my life. On the contrary I think it *relieved* one. In my opinion most children are very adaptable and if their feelings and concerns are observed and dealt with in a loving manner, there should not be any life-long problems. If my parents could make their divorce work relatively smoothly, then so should everybody else.

I have wanted to say this for a long time.

CONFLICTING RESEARCH

The study on the effects of divorce on children most frequently cited at present was done by Dr. Judith Wallerstein of the University of California at Berkeley. The study, which was based on 131 San Francisco area children, was published in 1984 and has often been used as evidence that divorce is indeed traumatic and harmful to children in the long term. Dr. Wallerstein was quoted by the press as saying about the ten-year study, "We have also seriously underestimated how much children and parents in divorcing families need help and most of all how many of them will continue to need help. We have been lulled by the notion that divorce is a brief crisis." Divorce according to the researcher can place a prolonged physical and emotional burden on children.

But in the last few years other researchers have found that the emotional and physical effects of divorce on children are not necessarily any more permanent than those of other major events, good or bad, which occur during the rise of all of us to adulthood. Two studies that were published in 1985, one American and one Canadian, both say virtually the same thing about the effects of divorce on children.

The 1.5-million-dollar American research effort, sponsored by the National Institute of Mental Health and published in 1985, compiled the research of seven long studies from different parts of the country and found that children of divorce revealed few health, emotional, or educational differences from those children who came from intact homes.

As part of the research that comprised the NIMH report, Martin Levin, of the Department of Sociology, Emory University, published a paper on the effects of "marital disruption" in children based on a sample of 8,000 children between six and seventeen from across the United States. He believes that much of what had been previously written on the subject of children and divorce is far from accurate:

> There is extensive but contradictory literature on the significance of the absence of one of the parents— generally the father—for such pathological effects upon the child as low school achievement, poor personal adjustment, gender role identification and dampened cognitive development. Divorce has been linked to stress and disequilibrium in the family and it is generally assumed that the process of divorce itself and the withdrawal of one parent is damaging to the child. On the other hand, a number of studies have found no relationship between parental absence and child development. The literature on the impact of marital disruption on child development is inconsistent, contradictory and inconclusive.

Levin goes on to criticize the method of much of the current research on divorce and children:

> Much of the research has failed to employ proper controls both in terms of variables which might directly affect the development of the child and those which might simultaneously affect the development of the child and the propensity of the parents to separate and divorce. A great majority of the studies tend to compare two-parent families directly with single-parent families. Few of the studies are based on national samples. Often only the children of disrupted parents are studied leaving comparison to non-disrupted families to be made implicitly. Even when comparison groups are included, the sampling designs employed tend to rely on captive

samples, (e.g. children in a particular elementary school, high school or university) or self-selecting samples such as families seeking counseling adjustment or participating in particular programs.

Levin also says:

> Divorce does not necessarily produce psychological damage in the child in every case. Other studies show that a happy one-parent family is less stress-producing for the child than an unhappy two-parent one and also, that children who appear to be distressed most by divorce are those with parents who continue to have turbulent relations following the divorce, or those who have been forbidden contact with the parent not in the home after the divorce.

Levin's opinion on the current state of the research and of the effects of divorce on children supports the findings of the research for *Solomon's Children,* even though the ages of those in the samples are somewhat different, as were the methods of obtaining information.

In a large study of 3,530 Canadian teenagers made by Project Teen Canada, sociologist Reginald Bibley and consultant Don Pasterski believe their results suggest "the great recuperative abilities of the human psyche which has been too long neglected in the handwringing about the evil effects of divorce." (One interesting statistic from this study was that 48 percent of the children answering the questionnaire said they got a "great deal" of enjoyment from their stereo, while only 44 percent felt that way about their relationship with their mother, and only 39 percent about their relationship with their father.) Perhaps it is the adults, then, who place so much importance on the value of intact family relationships, not the children. Or perhaps this importance is only recognized *after* the divorce.

PARENTAL WISH-PERCEPTION

As adults, we have glamorized the image of the blissful, in-
nocent days of childhood which may not reflect the reality of
our own childhoods but which makes a nice haven when
adulthood becomes a little too hectic. We as adults would
like very much to keep our perceptions of how happy our
childhood was or at least how happy it could have been
if only the right combination of events had been maintained.

Our popular image of childhood is a cross between
"Father Knows Best," *The Wizard of Oz,* and *Huckleberry Finn.*
On the one side we have the perfect family unit with loving
mothers and fathers and brothers and sisters supportive
of and interested in each other. On the other side we
have the mysteries and the magic of childhood with growth
and discovery unencumbered by parental influence or interference and where even the worst of experiences turn out
happily.

Neither image is very true to life. Most children are not
blissfully happy. They suffer stress, lose friends, worry about
success, sometimes experience the death of a loved one, and
during all this they are growing up—in itself a very difficult
and stressful event because of the physical, emotional, and
even social changes that mark their progress to adulthood.
Yet we adults treat them as though they had to be wrapped
in cotton wool when it comes to going through a divorce in
their family, even though, in the child's perception, the experience may be no more stressful than any one of a multitude
of childhood events. No matter what else may befall them as
children, good things and bad, we are convinced that divorce, and divorce alone, is responsible for any negative
changes we see in them, and also that these changes are
somehow permanent. Perhaps it is time for us to reassess our
opinions.

According to Mel Krantzler, divorce counselor and author of *Creative Divorce:*

> It goes without saying that children are enormously influenced by the quality of their family life and the relationship with their parents. However, short of actual neglect and physical abuse, children can survive any family crisis without permanent damage—and grow as human beings in the process—if they can sense some continuity and loving involvement on the part of their parents. While many parents may agree with this assertion in the abstract their confidence wavers in the first weeks and months after a divorce when they may see their own children so upset and unhappy. The agonies of the moment blind them to the potential for future well-being. Dr. Louise J. Despert, child psychiatrist and author of the outstanding book *Children of Divorce* [a book that has not received the attention it deserves], found that among all the troubled children she had treated or was consulted about, there were proportionally far fewer children of divorce than are found in the general population. Her conclusion is heartening to the many divorced parents who now wonder if they did the right thing: "It is not divorce, but the emotional situation in the home, with or without divorce, that is the determining factor in the child's adjustment. A child is very disturbed when the relationship between his parents is very disturbed. . . . Divorce then is not automatically a destructive experience. It may also be a cleansing and healing one, for the child as well as the adults. Divorce is not the costliest experience for a child. Unhappy marriage without a divorce . . . can be far more destructive.

In other words, for the child, divorce per se is not necessarily the big, bad event we usually make it out to be. But the way individual parents handle divorce can turn it into that.

THE DIVORCE INDUSTRY

The way we handle divorce today follows the letter of Solomon's wisdom, not its intent. We are still, even in these most civilized times, quite willing to sacrifice what is best for the child in favor of what is best for others. We subscribe to beliefs about the scarring influences of divorce on children because we have not readjusted our attitudes to fit the times. Furthermore, if we did not believe that children are ruined by divorce and that as many professionals as possible should therefore be on hand to help them cope, the system of divorce might not be so profitable for so many people. To put it bluntly, a lot of people earn a lot of money because of the way we have set up the process of divorce.

Over half a million lawyers (average salary, according to the *Journal of the American Bar Association*, $52,000 a year) and judges (salaries between $65,000 and $75,000 on average) spend some or all of their time on divorce and custody cases alone. Then there are those psychologists (salaries between $30,000 and $50,000), psychiatrists (average hospital salary, $56,000), social workers, counselors, etc. who come in afterward and are employed to pick up the pieces. The number of people employed in divorce and related industries is also on the rise. For instance, the number of welfare and agency workers, many of whom work directly in divorce-related situations, has doubled in the last decade.

And then there are those who study the aftermath of divorce. There has been a 250 percent increase in the number of Ph.D.s in psychology and the social sciences in the last fifteen years. The expenditures on social sciences and psychology research programs by colleges and universities were 641 million dollars in 1981—more than double what they were ten years before that. The federal government alone spent 656 million dollars for research in those areas in 1983. Is it any wonder that research reports continue to find damaging evidence about divorce? Few grants are given for research into the positive aspects of divorce.

There are also those who make their careers reporting on the whole process, and since most publications prefer to support the status quo because they think that is what the public wants to read, they continue to frame their reports on children and divorce in the same negative fashion they have done for decades.

For the most part we are presented with a negative view of divorce: It is seen as bad both morally, because it goes against the religious beliefs held by most of the population, and practically, because it interrupts the largest state of property ownership we have—marriage—and in doing so causes a good deal of chaos in the rearranging not only of a family's social life but of a family's financial life as well. So our structure of beliefs and myths helps us to dissuade people from getting a divorce, as does the process itself, which is arduous and unpleasant for everyone concerned, especially for the children.

FACING THE FACTS

Clearly, no matter how miserable a process we try to make divorce, we don't stop people from getting divorced. Perhaps, then, if we tried to make it a more tolerable experience, there would be fewer casualties. As it is, we encourage couples to remain in the cold and silent tomb of a dead marriage—where the epitaph reads, "for the sake of the children"—and we punish those who have the courage to go out and try again with a new spouse.

For anyone who has been there, it is no surprise that the presence of children from a first marriage is the main cause of divorce in a second marriage. And why is that? It is because we feel so guilty that we try to push broken marriages back together again, even when one or both partners are re-married, by using the children as bait. It seems that in searching for our own happiness we must sacrifice that of our children, and for that we must punish ourselves and our children.

We have been so busy in the last fifteen years worrying about the rising divorce rate and the terrible toll it is taking on the children, that we may not have noticed that the children are not doing so badly after all. While we have been feeding our guilt, many of these children of divorce have grown up, gotten married, and had families of their own, and their major regret about the whole situation is that we, the adults, handled it so badly. They don't care so much about the fact that their parents got divorced as they do about "the way" they got divorced.

What this book plans to show is that the "children of divorce" are not an army of walking wounded whose lives are laid waste by the ravages of divorce, but that this belief has been fostered and encouraged by interested parties not in the interests of the children but in the interests of the adults involved. It is time we exposed the layers of self-serving myth that have been built up around the idea of divorce and realized that we have been making it a difficult and often unpleasant process not for the sake of the children, but at their expense.

Chapter Two

The Children of Light

The way to do research is to attack the facts at the point of greatest astonishment.

Celia Green

The children of this world are, in their generation, wiser than the children of light.

I Timothy 16:8

I have always found that the best way to ascertain the truth about an issue is to ask those who are or were directly involved and not those who merely have an opinion on the subject. It is not enough to ask the adults involved in a divorce how their children feel or felt. It is not enough to ask the counselors and the psychologists who treat the emotional aftermaths of divorce. In order to find out how the children of divorce feel, it is necessary to ask the children themselves.

Therefore, to determine what the "children of divorce" really thought about the experience of their parents' divorce and how they feel it affected their later lives, I decided to ask children in as many states as possible and ranging in age from the young to the not so young, in order to get a good cross section of first-hand feelings and experience.

In order to get this cross section of Americans, I used

several different methods of finding potential participants. I asked columnists across the country who wrote about life and family issues to place requests in their columns for people over the age of twelve who wanted to participate in research for a book on children of divorce to contact me. In addition, I contacted various radio and television shows across the country and requested that they ask for volunteers. I also took out ads in the classified sections of major university newspapers asking for people to participate. The ad read as follows: "Author seeking people whose parents are divorced to interview for forthcoming book. Must be twelve years or older. Interviews confidential."

I kept the wording of the ad as nonspecific as possible in order not to indicate a particular attitude about divorce on my part. I did not want readers to think I was looking for respondents who had had generally positive or negative experiences or feelings. I deliberately gave no indication of my sex. However, I wanted to specify the age range, so people who were no longer technically "children" would feel free to respond, people who were old enough to express themselves clearly and on their own.

Because of the distances involved and in order to reach the maximum number of people as quickly as possible, I decided to gather information from the subjects by using a mail-out and return questionnaire—a method that had worked well for a previous study of this type that I had published, *Second Wife, Second Best?* Once the pool of possible respondents was achieved, the questionnaires were mailed out and I crossed my fingers that a large number would be returned.

THE QUESTIONNAIRE

The questionnaire consisted of 114 questions divided into four sections—The Separation, The Divorce, Remarriage, and Later On—plus a short section on biographical information at the beginning of the questionnaire. The questions came from discussions with people who had been through the divorce situation as children, from readings in the area, as well as from my own previous research. In order not to bias the respondents in favor of their mother or father, the terms "custodial" and "separated" were used in questions referring to their parents.

Many researchers would not attempt such a long mail-out questionnaire because response is notoriously poor for this type of research instrument. However, I felt that those who were truly interested in the subject would fill out the entire questionnaire and that, because of its length, it would cause them to think about their feelings and reflect on the various effects the divorce may have had on their lives more than if the questionnaire was shorter and could be answered quickly and with little effort. I had used a questionnaire of this length successfully before.

One of the reasons that this method may work so well for this type of research is that most of the questionnaires reach people whom no one has ever before asked how they felt about their situation. They have not, for the most part, been in therapy or counseling and few have known many other people who have been through what they have been through and with whom they could discuss things. For some of the older respondents it was the first time in the twenty or thirty years since their parents' divorce that they had been able to put down their feelings and know that someone would read them. For the younger ones, who had only recently been through the divorce of their parents, it was often the first time someone had shown an interest in how *they* felt

SOLOMON'S CHILDREN QUESTIONNAIRE

NAME: _____

AGE: _____

SEX: _____

MARITAL STATUS: _____

NUMBER OF CHILDREN: _____

OCCUPATION: _____

LEVEL OF FORMAL EDUCATION: _____

NUMBER OF TIMES MARRIED: _____

NUMBER OF TIMES DIVORCED: _____

AGE AT TIME OF PARENTS' DIVORCE: _____

NUMBER OF STEPBROTHERS AND SISTERS: _____

AGES OF STEPBROTHERS AND SISTERS: _____

TELEPHONE NUMBER: _____

PLEASE ANSWER THE FOLLOWING QUESTIONS. REMEMBER, THE PURPOSE OF THIS QUESTIONNAIRE IS TO ASCERTAIN YOUR FEELINGS AND EXPERIENCES RELATED TO BEING THE

CHILD OF DIVORCED PARENTS. BE AS SUBJECTIVE AS YOU LIKE AND FEEL FREE TO ILLUSTRATE YOUR POINTS WITH EXAMPLES WHEREVER POSSIBLE. GIVE AS MUCH DETAIL AS YOU CAN AND TRY TO AVOID SIMPLE YES OR NO RESPONSES. NOT EVERYONE WILL BE ABLE TO ANSWER EVERY QUESTION. YOUR ABILITY TO ANSWER SPECIFIC QUESTIONS WILL DEPEND ON YOUR PERSONAL CIRCUMSTANCES. THEREFORE, ANSWER ONLY THE QUESTIONS WHICH PERTAIN TO YOUR SITUATION. YOUR RESPONSES WILL BE KEPT CONFIDENTIAL. THE QUESTIONNAIRE IS DIVIDED INTO FOUR SECTIONS. EACH SECTION HAS QUESTIONS WHICH RELATE TO A DIFFERENT STAGE OF YOUR PARENTS' DIVORCE PROCESS. PLEASE NOTE THIS WHEN ANSWERING THE QUESTIONS AS SOME OF THEM APPEAR IN MORE THAN ONE SECTION.

THE SEPARATION

1) How did you first become aware that your parents were having marital problems?

2) How old were you?

3) How did you feel about this?

4) How did their friends and relatives react to your parents having marital problems?

5) How did these people react toward you at this time?

6) How did you cope with this change in your parents' relationship?

7) How did your brothers and sisters react at this time?

8) Were you closer to one of your parents than the other? Which one?

9) Did you ever feel that you were being asked to take sides?

10)   How did you cope with this?

11)   Did you have any idea why your parents were having marital problems?

12)   How long did this situation last before they separated?

13)   Which parent left the home?

14)   How did you feel at this time?

15)   How often did you see your separated parent?

16)   Did your parents continue to see each other and on what basis?

17)   How do you think they felt about each other at this time? About you?

18)   How would you say their relationship changed during the time of the separation?

19)   Did either or both of your parents explain to you what was going on at the time? How?

20)   Did they try to get back together at some point? Why? What happened?

21)   What did you hope would happen?

THE DIVORCE

22)   How did you feel when you found out your parents were getting divorced?

23) How did you find out?

24) Did either your parents or a court official ask you whom you wanted to live with?

25) Did they take your answer into account when deciding on custody?

26) How did you feel about their decision?

27) Did you blame either of your parents for the divorce? Why?

28) Did either of your parents begin to react differently towards you at this time?

29) Did your parents ever compete with each other for your attention, affections etc.?

30) What did you do?

31) Did either of your parents live with someone while waiting for their divorce?

32) How did you feel about this person?

33) Did either of your parents ever speak badly about the other parent's new relationships?

34) Do you think this influenced how you felt about the people involved? How?

35) What arrangements were made about you regarding holidays, birthdays or special occasions as a result of your parents being apart?

36) Did either of your parents discuss money with you during this time?

37) Did either of them ever suggest that you couldn't have some of the things you had before because of the divorce? What reasons did they give?

38) Did your custodial parent ever try to stop you from seeing your separated parent? Why?

39) What did you do about this?

40) What were your personal feelings about yourself at this time?

41) How did you feel about your parents?

42) What did you do on your custody visits?

43) How was this different from the time you spent with this parent before the divorce?

44) Did your custodial parent ever ask you to obtain gifts, money or information from your separated parent? If so, what?

45) Did either of your parents' reaction to the divorce make you uncomfortable. Why?

46) Did you know of any other children whose parents were divorced?

47) Did you ever think that your custodial parent may have been using your child-support money for reasons other than your support? If so, what?

48) Why do you think your custodial parent wanted custody of you in the first place?

49) How often did you see your separated parent?

50) Did you see more or less of this parent as time passed? Why?

51) Were any of your grandparents or aunts and uncles divorced? Who?

52) How much was your separated parent paying for child support at the time of the divorce?

53) Did this increase as time passed? How much?

54) At what age did you stop receiving child support?

55) Did your custodial parent contribute to your support? Approximately what percentage?

56) What arrangements were made re your extraordinary expenses (i.e., college tuition, camp, dental bills etc.)?

57) Did you ever contribute to your own expenses? If so, what percentage?

58) Did you ever feel that you were being denied anything as a result of your parents' divorce? What?

59) Did your separated parent ever fail to make support payments?

60) If so, did this affect your standard of living directly? How?

61) Did you ever try to get your parents back together? Why?

62) Do you think that your parents were basically honest with you about the divorce?

63) Did one of your parents hope that they would be able to get the marriage back together? Which one?

64) What did this parent do to try to achieve that?

65) Did you ever think that one or both of your parents "owed" you something as a result of the divorce? Why?

66) Do you think that your custodial parent's attitude toward your separated parent affected your own feelings for that person? How?

67) Did you miss your separated parent?

68) Did either of your parents ever speak badly of the other in front of you? If so, in what context?

69) How did this make you feel?

70) Were either of your parents physically violent with you or with each other? Explain.

71) Did you ever feel responsible for your parents' divorce? Why?

72) Please circle which of the following words best describes your feelings about your parents' divorce AT THE TIME?

guilty	relieved	normal
abandoned	pleased	interested
happy	indifferent	annoyed
secure	disloyal	blameless
threatened	sad	rejected
satisfied	content	anxious
different	important	embarrassed
puzzled	hurt	fortunate

REMARRIAGE

73) Did either or both of your parents remarry? Explain.

74) How did you feel about your stepparents?

75) How did you feel about your stepbrothers and sisters?

76) Did either of your parents have a child from the new marriage?

77) How did you feel about this?

78) Did you ever feel jealous or resentful of your step-parents or stepsiblings? Explain

79) Did either of your stepparents contribute to your support? How?

80) Did either of your stepparents want to adopt you?

81) How did you feel about this?

82) How do you think your separated parent felt about this?

83) Did you like one stepparent better than the other? Which one and why?

84) Were you ever conscious of using your parents' divorce or re-marriage to get your own way about something? Explain.

85) What would you say was the nature of the relationship between your custodial parent and your separated parent's new spouse?

86) How did this affect you?

87) Did you find that your attitude toward your parents' divorce changed after you got married yourself? How?

88) If you are divorced, how did you handle the situation with re-spect to your own children?

89) Did you think your parents and stepparents treated all the chil-dren the same or were some treated differently by one parent than another? Explain.

90) Why do you think this was?

91) What do you think are the major benefits of having a step-family?

92) What do you think are the major disadvantages of having a step-family?

93) Do you think your parents had any idea how you felt about the divorce before they did it?

94) Were they right in thinking that you felt that way?

95) How did your parents' divorce affect your relationship with other family members (i.e. brothers and sisters, grandparents etc.)?

LATER ON

96) Which one of your parents do you think you are most like as a person and in what way?

97) How do you feel about divorce in general?

98) How did your relationship with your parents change as a direct result of the divorce?

99) Do you think you would ever consider getting divorced?

100) What was the worst thing that happened to you as a result of the divorce?

101) Did your separated parent ever try to gain custody of you or steal you away?

102) How did you feel about this?

103) Did you ever want to go and live with your separated parent? Why?

104) What was the best thing that happened to you as a result of the divorce?

105) Would you rather your parents had stayed together until you had left home? Why?

106) Do you understand why your parents got divorced better now than at the time?

107) How do you think your parents could have handled the divorce situation differently?

108) How would you have handled the situation if it had been your divorce?

109) What is the relationship with your parents like now?

110) What is the relationship with your stepparents like now?

111) Would you say that it should be made easier or more difficult to get divorced in the future? Why?

112) What was the hardest thing for you to deal with re your parents' divorce?

113) Please circle which of the following words best describes your feelings about your parents' divorce NOW?

guilty	relieved	normal
abandoned	pleased	interested
happy	indifferent	annoyed
secure	disloyal	blameless
threatened	sad	rejected
satisfied	content	anxious
different	important	embarrassed
puzzled	hurt	fortunate

114) In the space remaining please add any additional thoughts or feelings you might have had about your parents' divorce and how it has affected your own life.

about the situation. In many cases the anonymity provided by this type of instrument allowed them to say what they really felt but could not perhaps have expressed to someone face to face.

I hoped that the open-ended nature of the questions would lead to some in-depth responses, carefully considered and thought out. Past experience had shown that this type of questioning, while it would be off-putting to anyone who was not seriously interested in thinking about what it meant to be a "child of divorce," would encourage those who were truly concerned to examine the depth of their feelings and experiences.

It took on the average about two to three hours to fill out the questionnaire, and in addition to that many people also wrote extra pages to further clarify their feelings or tell about particular instances that they felt were important.

Response was good from across the country, though it was slightly heavier from the east and west coasts and the south than from the plains states. Of the 1,050 questionnaires that were mailed out, 368 were returned. This 35 percent return rate was very encouraging.

WHO ANSWERED THE QUESTIONNAIRE?

The respondents came from thirty-two states in the United States and three provinces in Canada. They came from small towns and large cities, from farms and industrial areas. They were as young as eleven and as old as sixty-one.

Seventy percent were women and 30 percent were men. The higher representation of women is attributed to the fact that women are more interested in explaining how they feel about certain events and are generally more likely to be expressive of their feelings than men. Even so, those men who did reply put as much into their answers as the women, if not more. This may be attributed partly to the fact that, on the average, the male respondents were slightly older than the majority of the participants and therefore better able to express themselves.

The median time lapse between filling out the questionnaire and the occurrence of the divorce of their parents was five years. The shortest amount of time that had elapsed since the divorce was three years. The longest was forty-seven years. For most people, then, the divorce was still fairly fresh in their minds, though not so fresh they had not had time to sort out their feelings and impressions.

The average age of the participants *at the time of the divorce* was 11.4 years. The youngest was less than one year old when her parents were divorced and the oldest "child of divorce" was a man of twenty-five.

Their average age *at the time of response* was twenty-six. However, this is slightly skewed by the presence of a few people in their late fifties and early sixties. The median age, which was nineteen, was more representative of the majority of the sample.

Thirty-nine percent of the respondents were under twenty-one. This is convergent with the statistics for the general population, of which 34.4 percent is under twenty-one.

Of those over twenty-one, 51 percent were married or living with someone. This compares favorably with the general population, where 57.6 percent of those over twenty-one are in that domestic situation. Similarly, 12 percent of the respondents were currently divorced, compared to 11 percent of the general population in their specific age group.

Of those who were currently married, 23.5 percent had been married and divorced once before. This is only slightly higher than the general population where 19 percent of the married population has been previously divorced.

Forty-four percent of those who were married had

children of their own, compared to 47 percent of the general married population.

Forty-eight percent of the respondents had either step-siblings or half-siblings. Only 13 percent had half-siblings. The average number of step- or half-siblings was 2.67. However, some had as many as eight and others as few as one. The older the respondent, the more likely he or she was to have had a large number of step- or half-siblings. This is typical of the changing patterns in family size over the last half of this century.

In terms of age, 54 percent had all younger step- or half-siblings, 12.5 percent had all older, and 33.3 percent had some of each. However, the median difference in ages between the step- or half-siblings and those who filled out the questionnaire was only two years.

Some of the respondents were related to one another. For instance, there were two sets of husbands and wives as well as several mother and child sets who filled out the questionnaire because both of them were children of divorce.

Solomon's Children came from all walks of life and from a variety of educational and economic backgrounds. Following is a list of the occupations or educational level of those who responded to the question about occupation and education:

Student	Supervisor/Manager 11
High School 43	Waitress/Bartender 5
College 125	Designer 3
Graduate 20	Marketing 3
Secretary 25	Nurse 3
Homemaker 24	Banker 2
Salesperson 21	Bookkeeper 2
Teacher 16	Consultant 2
Self-employed 12	Printer 2

Teller	2	Filmmaker	1
Architect	1	Florist	1
Artist	1	Liaison Officer	
Auditor	1	(High School)	1
Caterer	1	Lawyer	1
Dancer	1	Publisher	1
Entertainment		Unemployed	6
Coordinator	1	Not listed	30

This sample represents a reasonable cross section of Americans. Major characteristics such as age, marital status, number of divorces, and number of children are convergent with the statistics of the population in general. The people who responded to the questionnaire for *Solomon's Children* could be your husband or wife, your parents, your friends or associates, or your children. What they have to say about divorce is not the opinion of a few but the thoughts of many.

"IT'S TIME SOMEONE HEARD OUR SIDE"

People may be curious about why anyone would want to spend three hours answering very personal questions for someone they don't even know who lives a long distance away. In order to give the reader some kind of feeling for the people who spent time and effort to help me write this book, here are some of their letters:

> *"Could you please send me two more questionnaires (one for each of my other two children). We have found that there were a number of misconceptions that my daughter had and the questionnaire has enabled us to become more aware and to discuss these things with her."*
>
> *California*

"I am writing in response to your ad about children of divorced parents. My husband and I both have divorced parents and we would be happy to help with the research because we think it's time someone heard our side."

New York

"I would like very much to be one of the people you select for your book Solomon's Children. *I am forty-three years old and come from divorced parents. For years I have felt something must be lacking in me as I feel I have suffered* little *or* no *trauma as a result of their divorce. Most of what I have read and people I have talked to insist that divorced children have a mountain of problems. What happened to me? In any case I look forward to reading your book."*

Arizona

"My parents have been divorced for five years resulting in major adjustments in my life especially moving to a town quite far away from my childhood community. Both parents are remarried now and most of the problems have been solved. I do have some convictions against divorce but must admit there have been some pluses too. I'd be willing to share any information with you."

Texas

"I am responding to your ad that asked for correspondence from children of divorced parents. I am a graduate student and my parents were divorced when I was eight years old. Your ad intrigued me because like most children from divorced parents I have numerous stories to share. I am interested in contributing to your research."

New York

"Please excuse the writing; I have just had surgery on my wrist and writing is difficult, but I wanted a chance to fill out the

questionnaire. There are so many things about my parents' divorce that I have never told anybody. It felt good to get it all on paper."

Illinois

"I am seventeen years old and a freshman at U.C.L.A. My parents have been officially divorced since I was about 7. I've also experienced other divorces through close friends and relatives. I would be happy to give you any kind of information on this topic in hopes that it will help others in the future in understanding a little more about marriage and divorce before it's too late."

California

"I am interested in your book on children of divorce. I have been through two divorces and I would like to share my experiences with you and others. I participated on a paper on divorced children when I was thirteen and now seven years later I find I have a much different perspective on the whole situation."

Colorado

"I hope my answers are helpful to you. I tend to become long-winded as I have a lot to say about my parents' divorce. However I tried to be precise to aid you in your interpretation of my answers. I found the questionnaire very interesting and I enjoyed filling it out. Through the written expression of my feelings I felt a sense of relief. It is always helpful to air quiet thoughts and emotions. Good luck in your research."

Arizona

"I would like to participate in your research about children of divorce. I believe my case is a little different as I was put in an orphanage before the divorce was final. I feel this affected my later life in the way I relate to my own children and my grandchildren."

Illinois

"Thank you for the questionnaire! It has been a real soul search for me."

Arkansas

"I hope you can read the writing. My mother said that I should just take my time and put down how I feel. You can use my name if you like."

Pennsylvania

"I am surprised how it was so easy to fill out the questionnaire. It may have been more difficult ten or fifteen years ago. Now that I have been divorced myself and am very happy to live without the negative parts of a relationship I am very satisfied and live mostly in the present. It all seems like very dusty history."

Michigan

This book has been written for all children of divorce, including those who wish their parents had done it sooner or with more elan, and for the parents who castigate themselves for their selfishness in wanting to find a happier life through divorce. It has been written to let the children of divorce finally have their say.

Chapter Three

The Rise of
the Child-King

The thing that impresses me most about America is the way the parents obey their children.

The Duke of Windsor

How many couples have suffered the agonies of a loveless or even violent marriage for the sake of their children? If, as I suspect, the number is huge, why did they place such importance on the well-being of their offspring, sacrificing their own happiness and safety to ensure it? We humans are not a species known for putting our children first and foremost, especially when they interfere with our own survival. There is burgeoning evidence, for instance, that female babies in China are frequently subject to infanticide because of the one child per family law being invoked there; many parents want a *male* child to take care of them in their old age, and they are not above sacrificing a female child, to try again for a boy. Perhaps, then, in recent decades we have romanticized our relationships with our children to excess, and perhaps, too, it suits our own ultimate goals to sacrifice our happiness for theirs.

In the last forty years the sacred status of the nuclear family as the only natural and "normal" family unit has been so heavily reinforced in our culture that many adults sacrificed their happiness and peace of mind in an ill-advised attempt to "stick it out" at least until their children were grown. Couples are therefore often still staying for a period of time in what is basically a name-only marriage until the children are independent or until they feel the children are old enough to understand.

This misguided effort to maintain the semblance of the traditional two-parent household was ostensibly done in order to provide the most normal and beneficial atmosphere for raising children. Later on we shall see that far from benefiting the children such situations are more likely to be detrimental, and the true motivation behind them is to benefit the parents, particularly the mother, as well as society in general.

When people maintain that they have forfeited a chance at a satisfying marriage with a more compatible adult in order to better raise their children, we often find that they have been acting to enhance a situation that was both acceptably conventional and personally self-serving. They are using the presence of their children to camouflage the gratification of their own needs, whether these needs be general social correctness or specific personal financial security.

Many people have yet to accept the fact that a good divorce is better than a bad marriage for everybody involved. The effects of a bad marriage on children, like those of a bad divorce, rather than being of a temporal nature can be reflected down through generations. It is not only the children forced to witness the gradual deterioration of their parents' relationship who will be affected, but their children as well.

If we really love our children, why do we not truly put their needs first, as we profess to do? Why do we not seek our mates on the basis of their parental potential rather than for their attractiveness, or status, or for other reasons that satisfy our own needs primarily? The answer may challenge many of our popularly held beliefs about parenthood.

Most of us were brought up to accept two very basic assumptions about family life—that all parents love their children, and that mothers are innately superior nurturers than fathers because they have "maternal instincts." Both assumptions have been exaggerated and encouraged by the press and other media, not to mention religious and political groups, over the last several decades. Women are usually portrayed as the "active" parents in commercials, films, and TV programs, men as the passive breadwinners of the family, occasionally baby sitting. Politically, issues that appeal to mothers, such as improved day care, are considered to be "women's issues," equating women with mothers. The strong hold of these popular stereotypes does not mean they are any more true than their antitheses—that all parents *don't* love their children, and that mothers are innately *inferior* parents than fathers.

THE CHILD IN RECENT HISTORY

To suggest that our instinct for loving and cherishing our children is overrated, and that adults should get on with their own lives and let children fit in where they can, is tantamount to blasphemy in our time. So much of modern society revolves around our belief in our innate desire to nurture and in the almost kinglike role of the child in this society.

But a look at our own past reveals no presence in humanity of an instinctive desire to raise children to a level of near godhood. Victorians sent their children to the workhouses of the time either because they could not feed them or because they just did not want them around. In the Far East a classic way of raising money for the family was to sell the younger daughter to a brothel. In some cultures—for instance, Australian aborigines and Eskimos— female children were so little valued that they were commonly exposed to the elements shortly after birth.

Yet in our era we focus on the child as the center of the culture, the center of the family, and the center of our relationship with each other. Not since the late eighteenth century, when the general practice of swaddling the infant ended and childhood hygiene and diet, including a return to breast-feeding, became a mother's foremost concerns, have we seen such a cult of child worship. Then, as now, the child was the focal point of all wisdom and all goodness. But this belief is the exception in human history rather than the rule.

The historical truth is, we have not always loved our children, or wanted them, or even liked them. The fact that children managed to exist at all was more a plan of nature than a plan of man during most of our history. The need to nurture children is not instinctive. It is an acquired state. Until this century, and in particular until after World War II, children were frequently seen as a nuisance and an inconvenience, when they were not being ignored entirely. This attitude was true not only of parents but of society at large. Women in particular have often been ambiguous in their feelings about children because their offspring have represented both a source of power and an agency of dependence for them. There has never been a time in our culture, then, when we did not secretly or overtly engage in some method of birth control, however primitive, in order to harness the power and curb the dependence. The fact that in Egypt in

1850 B.C. women would use a contraceptive concoction consisting of honey, soda, and crocodile excrement shows us just how long we have been concerned about *not* having children.

The reasons for our not wanting children have varied, depending on circumstances and social opinions. Children are expensive to raise; they often prevent a man from enjoying full use of his wife for significant periods of their married life; and until recently they have caused huge numbers of women to die in childbirth. Also they suggested to our ancestors their own mortality, marking inevitably the passage of time and reminding them that they could be replaced. How many stories have come down to us over the years of kings who wanted sons more than gold only to fear the loss of their kingdoms to them.

In the days before our own child-kings, most children were permitted to exist only if they could be "seen but not heard." Dickens has provided many good examples of how we regarded our offspring only a century ago.

But the Victorians seem almost sentimental about children compared to those who came before them. In fact, Dickens' depictions of the conditions of life and the general feelings for nineteenth-century children are positively utopian compared to those of some of his predecessors in the seventeenth century, such as the theologians Pierre de Bérulle and François de Sales, who described the state of childhood and especially infancy as "a beastlike state deprived of reason and judgement" or "the most vile and abject state of human nature, second only to death." It hardly seems that these men, who were respected thinkers in their time, could have been talking about the people who nowadays elicit squeals of joy from women and a proud puffing of the chest from their husbands (at least on television). Could they both be talking about—children?

Until the late eighteenth century a newborn child was not the beloved creature that we perceive today. Rather, he was some marginal life form replete with error and original sin. As such he was not a welcome addition to family life. In her book *Mother Love,* Elisabeth Badinter describes what often happened to children before the nineteenth century:

> Out of 21,000 infants born in Paris in the year 1780 fewer than 2,000 were kept at home under the care of their own mothers or live-in wet nurses. The other 19,000 were deported to distant parts of the countryside in appalling conditions having been handed often randomly to illiterate child-peddlers. . . . Once settled in their foster homes—rural hovels that would make Dickens' orphanages and Blake's satanic mills look like well-scrubbed nursery schools—the nurselings were usually fed an atrocious diet of wine-soaked bread and mashed chestnuts.

We must not think this behavior toward children was rare or deliberately abusive. Rather it was simply the great indifference of parents of all economic levels that led to such behavior.

Dr. Edward Shorter in *The Making of the Modern Family,* a history of family life, explains the following: "In the eighteenth and nineteenth centuries, parental indifference to infants was still firmly implanted among all segments of the popular classes and among all kinds of communities. At least that is what we must infer from the way the mothers treated their children. There was, for example, the cradle, in peasant hands a benumbing contraption. Wakeful children were commonly knocked into the sleep of insensibility. Most pernicious is the rural practice of . . . forcing children to go to sleep through immoderate rocking. . . ." Nor was violent rocking confined to peasants; in Vienna, "the dumb, harmful custom of calming children with benumbing shaking and rocking is still widespread among the lower classes." The same from Stuttgart: upper-class renunciation of the cradle for the crib, lower class persistence in "forceful shaking."

CHILDREN AS A RESOURCE

The fact that we did not necessarily love our children did not mean that we failed to make some good use of them. Next to slaves, they were the cheapest form of labor, and besides they were quite compact and fit into narrow places such as mines or chimneys where it was difficult for adults to go. Best of all, there seemed to be a never-ending supply of them.

Although it may not seem that we valued our children very highly if we treated them in what are today considered to be barbaric ways, we did find some worth in having them. We valued them then not for their childlike qualities or perfect innocence, but for how much additional income they could bring into the home.

Children took on commercial value in the late eighteenth century and came to be viewed as a potential economic resource. In 1770 Alphonse Didelo summed it all up nicely in *Instructions pour les sages-femmes,* where he said: "A State is powerful only insofar as it is populated. . . . Let the arms that manufacture and those that defend it be more numerous." As soon as this idea was well established, women were encouraged to "heed the voice of nature" and take up the role of breeding more potential "resources" as rapidly as possible.

Later, in the late nineteenth century, as mass-produced goods became the way of life in America, women began to lose their commercial value in the home. Since fewer and fewer of them were required to weave the cloth, make the bread, or wring the chickens' necks, their important task became to produce children. Motherhood became a woman's foremost responsibility. It was soon to become a vocation.

After the turn of the century, when women became even more free from standard domestic tasks because of an improving standard of living and more labor-saving devices in the home, they began to see motherhood not just as a bio-logical role in which they struggled to save as many children as possible from infant mortality, but as a role in which their talents could be put to use raising improved human beings.

But the change in our attitudes about women and children that most affects us now came after World War II. The emphasis on women as mothers became even more powerful at this time than it had been previously. One reason for this may have been that with so many men returning from the war in need of jobs, it was necessary to encourage the women who currently held those jobs to give them up and go back home where it was felt they belonged. One way of ensuring that they stayed there, leaving the jobs for returning G.I.s, was to see that they had as many young, dependent children as possible.

In order to make this a more attractive possibility to women, some of whom had held important and responsible jobs outside the home for several years, we elevated child-bearing and children to a level of importance that it had not enjoyed before. We turned it into a science and a profession, as well as an emotional commitment. The woman became the guardian of a precious commodity in whose tiny hands lay the future of the race or perhaps the world. To her we gave the enormous task of being the moral and educational mentor of the new generation. We made her feel hugely im-portant in this task by telling her that she was uniquely en-dowed to carry it out because of the perfect blending of her feminine instincts and her maternal nature.

For nearly twenty years after the war, the issues covered in women's magazines were those primarily relating to how to have a better baby. Dr. Benjamin Spock sold 28 million copies of his book on baby and child care alone. Children and their habits were examined by social scientists in minute detail. Every stage of a baby's development was cause for endless examination and discussion. The camera industry boomed as fascinated mothers and slightly overwhelmed fathers recorded every second of junior's progress for posterity.

Women were rewarded for this tireless devotion by being told (by Agnes Mayer in the *Atlantic*) that "no job is more exacting, more necessary or more rewarding than that of housewife and mother" and that "while women may have many careers they only have one vocation—motherhood."

Some people even went so far as to rethink woman's place in the educational system in relation to her most demanding role. "The task of creating a good home and raising good children should be raised to the dignity of a profession and made the primary purpose of women's colleges," said Anne Parnell, head of Sweet Briar College.

An article in *Life* magazine in May 1955, entitled "To Love, Honour, Obey and Study," discussed how campus marriage was becoming a way of life and gave helpful hints on how co-eds could juggle hubby, baby, and studying. They even invented a degree for those women who married and worked while their husbands went through school, at the same time dutifully having the requisite number of babies. Getting your P.H.T. (putting hubby through) was a big joke among graduate students on campuses at the time.

But it was no joke to the co-eds of the era. As one female teacher at a midwestern university was reported by *Life* magazine to have said in 1955: "Anytime I've got a senior [girl] who's not engaged, I know I've got a neurotic girl on my hands."

In fact, youthful marriages were encouraged by teachers and parents alike. A professor at Northwestern University noted: "I'd call it a great advantage to be married in college." A dean at M.I.T. commented: "The married students are a good influence on the community." And a doctor of obstetrics at Cornell University said: "These modern girls are simply marvelous in the biological sense. Even their pelvic measurements are better than their mothers'. Another thing is that they want to have babies. Lots of babies." Why wouldn't they, when the societal and familial pressures were so strong that not having children was tantamount to admitting that you were a failure as a woman or that you were neurotic? It was preferable to be an eighteen-year-old co-ed with a husband and baby. Everyone was reinforcing the idea that the truly feminine woman was also the truly maternal woman. So much so that even those women who may have had their doubts gave in and took up the torch of motherhood. A whole generation of women was sacrificed to raising and nurturing their child-kings regardless of their own needs and personalities. The press, the intellectuals, the politicians, all took part in encouraging women to do this. But no one really questioned the motives or the validity of these young marriages at the time. According to Betty Friedan, in *The Feminine Mystique:* "The millions of American youngsters who in the 1960's were marrying before they were twenty, betrayed an immaturity and emotional dependence which seeks marriage as a magic short-cut to adult status, a magic solution to problems they cannot face themselves. These infantile brides and grooms were diagnosed as the victims of this generation's 'sick, sad love affair with their own children. ' "

After World War II the idea of *Kinder, Küche, Kirche,* which had first surfaced in Nazi Germany and stressed woman's only true role as her biological role, was reinforced across the Western world, but the message was especially strong in the United States. Women's magazines at the time were leading the parade with articles like, "Have Babies While You're Young," "Don't be Afraid to Marry Young," "Training Your Daughter to Be a Wife," and "Cooking to Me Is Poetry." No matter what the subject matter, it was filtered for female consumption through the woman's role of mother or housewife. Even famous women who were written about at the time were not written about because of what they had done but only in terms of their lives as wives and mothers. An editor of *The Ladies Home Journal* said: "If we get an article about a woman who does anything adventurous, out of the way, something by herself, you know, we figure she must be terribly aggressive and neurotic."

Even in the late seventies, there was a profusion of articles in women's magazines across the country on breast-feeding, natural childbirth, and the damage done by working mothers.

THE CHILD AS A CONSUMER

Is it any wonder that, with all this pressure to become mothers and only mothers, the women who succumbed would value perhaps too highly the only product they were allowed to create—children? Children of the fifties and sixties were indulged or perhaps over-indulged in ways their parents could never have dreamed of when they were young. Everything was done "for the sake of the children." Whole new industries sprang up to service them. New educational policies were implemented to encourage their development. New social theories evolved to help us try to understand them. Children were infinitely fascinating to parents and to society. We became child crazy.

While we said that what we were doing was intending to create a better life for our children, there were other motives at work that we kept to ourselves.

Between 1946 and 1964, 76 million children were born in the United States. They became known as Baby Boomers, and because of their numbers they became a very important force in every aspect of our society. They accounted for nearly one-third of the population by 1980. So the major thrust of our economy's mass production techniques was aimed at them, and for the last twenty to thirty years they have been our biggest market.

It was nearly fifty years ago, in 1938, when the Fair Labor Standards Act was passed, that public outrage won out over commercial interest in the United States and child labor came to an end. (The act, amended in 1961, forbade the employment of children under sixteen in heavy industry, transport, and commerce.) Now we have arrived at a point where we need our children not for what they can produce but for what they can consume.

Historically, our society has equated population growth with prosperity and success. More children means more consumers, which means a healthy economy. One hundred years ago the average American family had five children. Today the count is down to two. This has some economic theorists worried, and their concern is not surprising when you examine the child as a consumer.

One of the largest areas of consumption for a child is education. Between 1960 and 1982 the federal outlay for education and related activities increased 1,500 percent. Three and one-half million teachers are employed, essentially by the children of this country, on the elementary and secondary levels alone. Childhood education is very big business. But it is nothing compared to some of the other businesses that base their entire existence on the presence of large numbers of children and willing parents.

Between 1975 and 1982 television executives increased their advertising budget for toys by 120 percent, to 220 million dollars. In 1982 nearly 4 billion dollars was spent on records and tapes. The previous year saw the snack products industry aimed just at teenagers shoot past the 6-billion-dollar mark. For Christmas 1984 alone, 17 million Cabbage Patch dolls were sold—that is almost one doll for every American child under the age of five. But perhaps the happiest manufacturers at the moment are the ones who produce video games and related materials. Between 1977 and 1982 the home video market increased by 1,900 percent. Industry revenues from the sales of video-related products were a staggering 3.5 billion dollars.

Under the circumstances, is it any wonder that we regard our children as such special creatures? They are probably our best consumers, and as long as we encourage their parents to indulge them, they will continue to be a powerful force in determining our gross national product.

THE CHILD AS A POLITICAL FORCE

On another level, there is the geopolitical argument that favors large numbers of children. Population growth has been a driving force in the United States economy for over three centuries. More people pay more taxes, but not all government expenses have risen proportionately. There are, therefore, significant amounts of money left over to spend on things such as space exploration or world domination. Furthermore, world power and population growth are connected: You cannot be a world power with a smaller population than other potential powers. It is estimated that to be a world power these days a country needs at least 100 million people and a growth rate to match its rivals to maintain its position in the world balance of power. The only four countries still growing at an undiminished rate are China, India, Pakistan, and Indonesia. As the theory goes, unless the United States keeps up its human production quota, it will soon lose status as a world power to those countries with significantly higher populations.

"FOR THE SAKE OF THE CHILDREN"

For these and other reasons there is still considerable pressure on women to produce babies. Now that they have some say over whether to have children or not, the biological accident method of population enhancement is not as powerful as it once was. However, the psychological enhancement method is still going strong. The social and psychological pressures put on women to have children are tremendous, and perhaps even more insidious than they have been in the past. Even women who are perfectly happy in a childless marriage can succumb to the rigorous and often unrelenting pressures to have children:

> The eight years before we had children were glorious. I had an enjoyable career, an idyllic home life. But friends pitied us, undoubtedly worried that we would continue living hedonistic, meaningless but terribly comfortable lives unless we became parents. When we started a family therefore it did not occur to us that we were just succumbing to the social pressures and the media. Now we see that all this couldn't have failed to condition us.

So said Shirley Radl, President of the National Organization For Non-Parents in 1972.

Many of the women whose mothers had children in the fifties, and became the first of the post-war mothers to embrace children as a raison d'être, are now having children of their own, and they, too, are duly convinced that the only way to have true happiness and fulfillment is to become a mother. And so they go ahead and have children, feeling that they are satisfying not only a need but a right. This puts a great deal of pressure on these children to fulfill their mother's desires for personal contentment. By placing unrealistic expectations on our experience as parents, we also put these same unrealistic expectations on our children as well.

In order for parenting to be able to fulfill and satisfy us more than any other life experience, we must perceive our children as appropriately powerful, even magical, creatures. In essence they are our kings, for while we may protect and serve them we also seek the satisfaction of our present and the continuity of our future from them.

Between our own needs and those of society itself we have elevated our children to a level far beyond what nature intended and one that is not in their best interests in the long run. We have made them kings, but the price we demanded from them is high. We have demanded that they give us joy and a reason for living, although both of these can come only from within ourselves. Many parents hold their children to this implied promise and wring their happiness or ostensible happiness from the battered personalities of their own children. We say that we love our children and that is why we cherish them to the point of godhood. But do we really? Are we not just masking our own needs and desires to have power over each other in our exhortations of emotional attachment to our children? Or perhaps even worse, are we not holding them responsible somehow for the mistakes of our own lives, and do we not perhaps punish them unconsciously for existing?

If we truly loved our children, we would make the decision of the true mother in the Solomon story and think only of their interests. However, the majority of those involved in the divorce process today are only too happy to agree to sacrifice the children for the needs of the parents or of the state, all the while saying they are acting "in the best interests of the children."

We have set up a pattern in the divorce and custody process that is as ridiculous as the routine in the early days of this century when children of divorce automatically went to the father because they were regarded as his property. We continue to follow procedures for divorce and custody that were made more than a generation ago, inflicting the feelings and opinions of those who made them on a generation that was just being born at the time.

Just as much as staying together "for the sake of the children" is often more selfish than self-sacrificing, suiting the needs of the parents above all, so is the current system of getting divorced. Again the children are caught in the middle. We are still telling ourselves that what we are doing is right, and that they are too young to understand, they cannot cope, they would be traumatized, or whatever other excuse we can think of for getting our own way. Then we turn around and say that divorce is bad because of what it does to the children, when what we are actually doing is transferring our own inability to deal with the situation onto them. It is not what divorce does to the children but what we do to the children in the name of divorce that is wrong.

Chapter Four

The Motherhood Myth

I cannot think, offhand, of any civilization except ours in which an entire division of living men has been used, during wartime, or any time, to spell out the word "MOM" on a drill field.

Philip Wylie

In an ideal world, both parents would have an equal, if different, contribution to the shaping of their offspring. In some cultures the parental participation in the child's upbringing is divided along the lines of sex—with the father taking responsibility for male children and the mother, the female children. In other cultures it is age that determines which parent has the major influence, with mothers generally taking the major responsibility for infants and small children and fathers taking over around the time of puberty. In each type of culture both parents have a significant role in shaping the child into an adult. Such is not the case in our culture.

In 1983, 5.8 million children in the United States lived in one-parent households. In close to 90 percent of those households the one parent was the mother. Most of these children see little of their natural fathers for a variety of reasons that will be discussed later in the book.

The amazing thing about this situation is not so much that it exists but that we have encouraged it to exist. Most people still think that children are actually better off with their mothers, often exclusive of their fathers, and so the courts continue to judge custody cases accordingly. Why? Why have we come to a point were we can disallow fathers as important, significant contributors to their children's lives and in doing so shift the entire burden for child rearing onto mothers, many of whom are staggering under the weight of this often unwanted responsibility? The answer is fairly simple.

Over the years we have built up a perception of motherhood that is not only unreal but unfair. For every point we have given to mothers as parents we have subtracted one from fathers, until we have reached the point at which divorced mothers are seen as parents and divorced fathers are seen as little better than impregnators with no real interest in their progeny.

The myths that surround motherhood can appear wholesome, especially when linked with love of God and country, not to mention apple pie. How can you not love motherhood when it keeps such great company? But there are some situations in which the myths about motherhood can be harmful. Divorce is one of them.

MOTHERS AND DIVORCE

Situations such as the one described in the opening quote of this chapter are indicative of the lengths to which our society is willing to go to emphasize our dedication to the idea of motherhood. On the one hand we idolize mothers with public displays of sentiment, and yet on the other there is an often unspoken or implied belief that mothers by and large are responsible for many of the problems that children carry with them through adulthood. The Freudian concept of motherhood, which has proved very popular in North America in the last fifty years, links the mother's neurotic need to be self-fulfilled, as a person rather than just as a mother, with the psychological and physical ills that later befall her children. Oedipus conflict and penis envy became catchwords of an era, and at the center of the entire problem, at least as far as the Freudians were concerned, was mother. Fortunately, we have begun in recent years to move away from Freud's ideas about women in general, and the validity of Freud's theories on mothers is not the issue here. What is at issue is how divorced mothers can have a deleterious effect on their children, both during childhood and through adulthood, because of their own difficulties in coping with divorce.

A recent study published by Robin Akert of Wellesley College indicated that in the break-up of a relationship women fare much worse than do men. According to the study women feel more guilty, more unhappy, more lonely, more depressed, and particularly more angry. They also have more trouble with physical manifestations of stress such as overeating or undereating and the use of alcohol or drugs. In addition, they find it more difficult to form new relationships and take about twice as long to remarry as do divorced men. Yet we still feel that while they are under all this stress mothers make the best and often the only proper parents!

In a study done in 1980 at the McMaster University School of Social Work, researcher Michael Wheeler found a close link between a woman's age at the time of marriage and her ability to cope with divorce. Fifty-six percent of the women in his study married before the age of twenty. Those women who married younger than the average age had significantly higher levels of post-separation or post-divorce depression. Wheeler attributes this phenomenon to the fact that women who were very young at the time of marriage had not clearly developed their identities. "They may have believed that marriage will give them a role to play and a purpose in life which they have not otherwise been able to find. Conceivably, the more marriage has been invested with hopes of giving meaning to life, the more acute the sense of depression is likely to be upon its dissolution." Wheeler goes on to say that a key factor in how well children handle separation and divorce is the mental health of the custodial parent. "The parent with custody is expected to be an ever present resource and guide in meeting the children's needs and to do this without the support of another adult; the task is onerous at the best of times, it is even more onerous—and the consequences to the children likely to be more severe—when the mental health of the single parent (the mother in most cases) is under stress."

Over 65 percent of the respondents to the *Solomon's Children* study had some very negative things to say about their mothers. It was not that they necessarily had stopped loving them, but having observed their behavior in the divorce situation Solomon's Children certainly began to change their minds about liking them. The following is a quote from a twenty-two-year-old girl who was eighteen when her parents divorced:

> *"I began to lose my respect for my mother. She went from being placed on a pedestal in my mind to being just an average person with too many faults and bad character traits that I hated. I still loved her because she was my mother but I did not like her any more. She went out of her way to make my life miserable. She became hostile and resentful toward me. She'd make me feel guilty and ask me to justify my father's actions. Telephone conversations with her always ended in tears—mine. She made the entire process of divorce and what came after into pure hell for me*

and my father. This put a wall between us that still exists today.
She was constantly trying to persuade me of my father's awful-
ness and force me to leave him and come and live with her. I
think she felt that if she could not have him then neither could I.
When that did not work she succeeded in driving my family
away from me with cruel lies about how I was responsible for the
divorce. To date I have relatives who won't acknowledge my ex-
istence. The worst thing about the divorce was that I lost the
love of many of my relatives and that I saw my mother for the
person she really was."

One of the worst experiences of divorce for a child is
watching the pedestal that has supported his or her mother
begin to crumble. For then the child must question not only
his own feelings about his mother, but society's as well. How
could this woman who tucked him into bed at night and
held him in her arms softly cooing him to sleep be the same
one who asks him to spy on his father when he goes for a
custody visit? The child is left to question his own young
perceptions about mother and try to reconcile the two
images of her that are being presented to him. It is an unfortunate truth that in analyzing the situation the child often
finds the mother wanting.

MATERNALISM, THE STATE, AND SOCIETY

We have written endless songs about mother, dedicated
things to her, painted innumerable portraits of her, idolized
her in every way, even had her tattooed on ourselves. We
have placed mother in a realm of super beings (often without
her consent), and in doing so we have replaced a woman and
a person that once existed with a deified essence of
maternalism that at once succors us and controls us.

Somehow when women become mothers they stop

being perceived as the people they were before. This transmogrification is inflicted on some and used by others to achieve special status. Back in the seventeenth century, women accused of crimes for which execution was the usual method of restitution had recourse to "Pleading Their Bellies" if they were pregnant. They could delay the fateful day for as long as they were pregnant. Needless to say there were a lot of pregnant women in the jails of the time. Some managed to delay the date with the executioner for years just by making sure they stayed pregnant.

More recently, in the United States a grandmother, Velma Barfield, who had been accused and found guilty of murdering, among others, her own mother, was finally executed according to the laws of her state after years of appeals. If the person involved had been a grandfather instead of a grandmother, would the delays have gone on so long? Would the press have gone to such great lengths to point out the familial status of the convicted murderer? Men, it seems, still maintain their previous position and add to it the persona of father, but women become mothers first and people second.

Most of us have been brought up to believe that the attitude about motherhood that prevails in our society is not only right and proper but good. But it is not right to judge a woman solely on her ability as a maternal agent any more than it is right for a woman so judged to wreak vengeance for this captive state of her children. According to feminist Betty Friedan, it works like this:

> . . . it is because the mothers' dreams which their children are acting out have become extremely infantile. These mothers have themselves become more infantile and because they are forced to seek more and more gratification through the child, they are incapable of finally separating themselves from the child. Thus, it

would seem it is the child who supports life in the
mother in that "symbiotic" relationship and the child is
virtually destroyed in the process.

And this is how author Juliet Mitchell sees the situation:

> At present, reproduction in our society is often a kind of
> sad mimicry of production. Maternity is often a carica-
> ture of this [work]. The biological product—the
> child—is treated as if it were a solid product. Parent-
> hood becomes a substitute for work, an activity in
> which the child is seen as an object created by the
> mother, in the same way that a commodity is created
> by the workers. . . . No human being can create another
> human being. The child as an autonomous person inev-
> itably threatens the activity which claims to create it
> continually merely as a possession of the parent. The
> child as possession is supremely this. Anything the child
> does is therefore a threat to the mother herself who has
> renounced her autonomy through this misconception of
> her productive role. There are few more precarious
> ventures on which to base a life.

We have expected the women in our society, in the last
several generations at least, to give up being autonomous individuals and to devote, sacrifice, and forfeit themselves for
the sake of their children. We have told them this is what
they were born for. We have reinforced this so strongly that
today women still see this role as their only true purpose in
life.

But the price for this reproductive slavery is now being
exacted. It is a high one. In relegating a large number of
people to a very narrow existence with little to focus on outside of that existence, we have inadvertently also provided
them with a power base, and by building on this power base
they have been able to wield control over others.

MATERNALISM AND POWER

Once, when women and men married for life and the breeding of children took up most of a woman's adulthood, there was little time to argue or to jockey for positions of power either within the marriage or within the culture. Making a living took all the energy most people had. But now women have more time and more social permission to secure their positions. The fight for might on the home front is a relatively new phenomenon. It has received a boost from the popular press, which has taken to championing the side of women, especially mothers, and women have used the voice of the feminist movement to shout down their husbands on domestic issues. Their battle cry is, "But what about the children?" It has become an amazingly effective slogan in recent years, especially for mothers asking for something from the state or from their children's fathers. The idea that one has or possibly might have children at some point has proved very useful both as an excuse for not doing some things and as a method of getting permission to do others. Evidence of this is seen in the growing trend to increased maternity leaves. Once upon a time six weeks was seen to be enough. Now many unions insist on longer maternity leaves, even as long as seventeen weeks, as part of their benefit package demands. There has even been some consideration given to maternity leave for adopting parents and to paternity leaves. Such measures may be progressive, but they are not productive.

The cry of "But what about the children?" is echoed most strongly by divorcing mothers. But the stereotype of the middle-aged woman left to raise her brood alone and unaided is an inaccurate exaggeration of the true picture of the divorcing mother, who is, statistically speaking, more likely to be in her late twenties with one or possibly two children. But since these women are fighting for power from a supposedly powerless position, we tend to turn a blind eye when they use the one weapon that is at hand—their children. If the children get caught up in the struggle and become victims of their mothers' quests to get some control over their relationships with the rest of the world, then so be it.

Most divorced mothers would never admit to using their children to gain control over their ex-husbands or over the state. But the children often perceive themselves as being the rope in the tug of war between their parents. They also see themselves as the bait that their mothers have dangled in front of their fathers to try and get them to return to the marriage:

> "My parents saw each other frequently. They even tried to reconcile 'for the sake of the children.' This was the line my mother always used to get my father to come back. She tried to make him feel quilty. It worked for about two months and then he left again. I think he realized that it was all a ploy on my mother's part. She had just lost a chance to marry the man she had left Dad for and I think it really hit her how alone she would be now."

The children are not always used just as a bartering tool in the contest that often follows a divorce. Sometimes they are also manipulated as part of more insidious means used to gain power either over the children themselves or over others through them. One respondent wrote:

> "My mother told me on various occasions that my father 'beat her,' 'poisoned her,' had 'gone out with a prostitute,' 'beat me,' 'raped her' and that he would rape me too if he ever found me alone. I currently believe it was all a lie. In the thirty years he was married to my stepmother he never did any of those things. I

don't think he was capable of doing them ever. I do think that she was trying to get me to stop loving him though."

Another commented:

"My mother started drinking when we moved away from her hometown. She didn't want to move and kept pressuring Dad to go back but he couldn't because of his job. By 1980 she was drinking heavily. She became an alcoholic. And so I stayed with her to help her with her drinking problem while my sister went to live with my father. She kept saying that when I was old enough to look after myself she would die. And she did."

MOMISM, U.S.A.

The term "momism" was coined in 1943 by Philip Wylie in his *Generation of Vipers*. It refers to the widespread social phenomenon of "mother worship." In Wylie's opinion this excessive adoration of mother symbolizes a pathological emptiness in women's lives. With nothing else to occupy them women prey on their children, smothering them with affection so they will remain tied to the home. Mother worship is ostensibly based on the endless self-sacrifice of "mom" but in reality it is rooted in her insatiable appetite for devouring her young and preventing them from developing into independent adults.

In *Their Mothers' Sons* (1946), Dr. Edward Strecker, a consultant to the Surgeon General of the Army and Navy and one of Wylie's contemporaries, also found mom to be at fault. The majority of the almost 3 million men who were found unfit for military service in World War II lacked maturity, "the ability to face life, to live with others, think for

themselves, and stand on their own two feet." According to
Strecker,

> A mom is a woman whose maternal behavior is moti-
> vated by the seeking of emotional recompense for the
> buffets which life has dealt her own ego. In her relation-
> ship with her children, every deed and almost very
> breath are designed unconsciously but exclusively to
> absorb her children emotionally and to bind them to
> her securely.
>   . . . the emotional satisfaction, almost repletion,
> she derives from keeping her children paddling about
> in a kind of psychological amniotic fluid rather than
> letting them swim away with the bold and decisive
> strokes of maturity from the emotional maternal
> womb. . . . Being immature herself, she breeds immatu-
> rity in her children and by and large they are doomed
> to lives of social insufficiency and unhappiness. . . .

These two men were perhaps the first ones to give a
name to a situation that the respondents saw all too clearly.
Underneath the surface of self-sacrificing motherhood were
all manner of self-serving motivations. One of the most star-
tling things that the respondents had to say, whether they
were men or women, still children or already senior citizens,
was that they did not subscribe to the popular myths of
motherhood. Their opinions differed vastly from the commonly held conception of the nurturant, selfless, loving creature that is generally associated with the term "mother."
They may have understood their mother's behavior, they
may have forgiven it, but they did not like it or wish to emu-
late it. They were determined to avoid acting in a similar
fashion with their own children. Most were extremely embarrassed by it. And many felt that their mothers had used
them in an emotional tug of war with others regardless

of the negative effect it was likely to have on their lives. For example:

"I can remember it so clearly even now and it's over thirty years ago. I was ten. It was a long weekend in the summer and most of the people on our street were outside. My father had packed his bags in the family car and was preparing to drive away. They had been fighting for months and he had finally had enough. She told him to get out. My mother then decided she did not want him to go after all, and she threw herself over the front of the car and windshield to stop him. All the neighbors were watching as they went down the street like that. He drove away braking and lurching the car to throw her off. Both of them disappeared for several days leaving me to myself. I thought I would die of embarrassment."

These "children of divorce" have seen another side of motherhood. Not the loving, doting, sacrifice-everything-for-the-children mother that we have mythologized so completely, and inaccurately, but a woman often trapped by circumstances, powerless, angry, who will use whatever she can to get revenge or to aid her own survival:

"My mother used to scream and throw things at my father. Once she attacked him with a butcher knife when he came to pick us up. After that we didn't see him as often and he never came to the house again."

"My mother used the children to keep my dad in line after he left her. She knew he felt guilty about leaving and so she played up to his guilt all the time. When my sister got pregnant in high school she blamed it on my father. Every time something went wrong with one of us she blamed him. They went on like that for ten years, married but not married. My brothers and sister still

hate my father but I can see that most of their feelings are the result of what my mother did not of who he was."

"My mother couldn't stand the fact that I loved my stepmother. Once she went to the place where she worked and physically attacked her. She used to write her nasty letters and when I would come back from seeing her and my father she would say to me thing like, 'So you've been visiting that whore again.'"

EXAMINING THE INSTINCT ISSUE

"The notion that maternal wish and activity of mothering are instinctive or biologically predestined its baloney," according to the writer Betty Rollin. "Try asking most sociologists, psychologists, psychoanalysts, biologists—many of whom are mothers—about motherhood being instinctive; it's like asking department-store presidents if their Santa Clauses are real."

One of the greatest defenses for the idea of mothers as superior parents was the belief that women possessed a maternal instinct that made them uniquely capable of wanting and raising children. In order to give credence to this idea of universal maternal instinct, those who encouraged belief in it would point to the animal kingdom as an example of the female need to procreate and nurture, to obey the call of nature. The animals of the wild were thought to exemplify the true state of maternal instinct at its highest level because their procreative and nurturing behavior was untouched by personal interest or selfish needs. However, human mothers are not animals of the wild. They do have very personal interests and needs. Children often get in the way of these. If one were to accept the idea of universal maternal instinct, then it would be difficult to understand why, for instance, there are 10 million children living on the streets of Brazil's cities after being cast out from their homes. And Brazil is supposedly a conservative, Catholic country. Closer to home, the existence of a deeply ingrained maternal instinct makes it hard to understand why several billion dollars a year are spent on birth control research in order to let women prevent conception. It is even more difficult to justify the fact that there were just over 4 million live births in the United States in 1983 and 1.5 million abortions. Forty-two percent of these abortions were for women who already had one or more children. Surely if there was such a thing as universal maternal instinct, none of these situations would be necessary.

It is interesting to note that even though in art, literature, and the popular press we place such high import on motherhood, as a nation we do not rate it as a major priority in attaining human happiness. A 1976 nation-wide survey done by Columbia University asked a group of more than 52,000 Americans ranging in age from fifteen to ninety-five what they thought were the things in life that would most likely make them happy. Being a parent turned out to be much less important for both men and women than expected. Things like health, personal growth, social life, success, and recognition were all weighted as far more significant in terms of being happy. For married women, being a mother rated in tenth position on the overall happiness scale.

Also in 1976, advice columnist Ann Landers conducted a survey among her readers. She asked the question, "If you had to do it all over again, would you have children?" Seventy percent of the 10,000 women who responded said "No!" In 1984, Charles Westoff, director of Princeton University's Office of Population Research, projected that 25 percent of women now in their twenties would remain childless by choice. But what about the other 75 percent?

The fact is, a lot of women don't like children. Many have children because they are pressured into it either by society or by families, or because children are a source of revenue, or because they themselves are duped into believing that somehow their maternal instinct will take over when the children are born and they will love and nurture them, or because they get careless. Sometimes they are afraid not to have children because of the social sanctions that await women who choose to remain child-free. How many of these women are cajoled, forced, intimidated, or pressured into motherhood?

Nevertheless, we continue to insist that most women make better parents for their children than their husbands, and we hand over custody to women regardless of their true motivations for being mothers in the first place and regardless of the behavior that may have been generated by it.

"My mother always talked abut how awful my dad was, but my dad never spoke ill of her. Until one day when I hung up talking to her and my dad was living with me. He said, 'I'm sick and tired of pretending I don't hate your mother, when I do.' He then told me how she had been promiscuous (funny but I knew it all along) and he had caught her at it. He told me how she had tried to abort me twice—first with castor oil, then with a hat pin. And how when she knew she was in labor with me she sent the doctor away hoping that I would die in the birth. If my father hadn't been there to deliver me I probably would have."

"I felt completely abandoned by my mother because she wouldn't talk to me, she was so interested in her new boyfriend. Everything was what he wanted. Pride and tradition forced her to take me, that and companionship. She thought she would be all alone without Daddy, but when she met Fred she didn't need me that much any more."

"My mother succumbed to social pressures to have custody of me. She didn't want people saying she was a bad person because she didn't want to look after her own child."

"Even though my mother took me from my father I never had a place in her life. She was a performer and in her circle it was fashionable in those days not to have children, so even when I was a young child she used to tell people that I was either a cousin or adopted, depending on the circumstances. She perpetuated this fantasy till the day she died and never acknowledged me to her friends as her child."

"My mother used to ask me to tell everyone that I was her younger sister. She didn't want them to know that she had a daughter in case it made her look old."

"My mother took me so that my father couldn't have me. I was six or seven at the time. That was forty-five years ago. She died three years ago and even on her deathbed she told me how much she had always hated me."

According to Margaret Mead, "there is no evidence that suggests women are naturally better at caring for children than men." It appears that in our need to reassure ourselves of the validity of the myths of motherhood we have overlooked the fact that some people are not well equipped to be parents and others are. The sex of the parent is not necessarily the factor that decides the presence or absence of that which we like to call "maternal instinct."

WITH QUIET CONSENT

There were no questions about incest or child abuse included in the questionnaire because it was thought that if such events had occurred and were an important memory of the respondents they would provide the information in answers to such questions as "What was the worst thing that happened to you as a result of divorce?" But there were enough women who volunteered information of this nature to make me want to include a short section on incest in this chapter because they all placed the bulk of the blame on their mothers:

> *"The hardest thing I had to deal with with respect to my parents' divorce was the sexual molestation by my grandfather and my mother's two boyfriends. Both of her boyfriends beat and molested me. I am sure that she had an idea of what went on but then she thought she was going to marry both of them and so she clammed up. As a teenager I became deathly afraid of her and began to hate her for what happened. Interestingly enough she didn't end up marrying either one of them. In fact she never remarried at all."*

> *"My stepfather was an educated Archie Bunker. He used to make sexual advances to me when I was in my early teens and he would verbally abuse me as well. She did nothing to interfere even after I told her what he was up to. Later he left her for a much younger woman, someone just a little older than me."*

Much of the literature on families in which incest takes place has begun to examine the role of the mother as a causative factor in the situation. Experts generally describe her as a cold and unloving woman who rejects not only her husband but also her children. She is judged particularly deficient in maternal love. In addition, she is seen to be infantile in her personality and often pushes her daughter into the role she wishes to abdicate, including the sexual relationship with the father or stepfather. Several clinicians categorize these mothers as passive-dependent personalities. Richard Sarles, for example, in *Father-Daughter Incest*, observes of incestuous families, "Wives tend to be immature and infantile individuals who are passive and strongly attached to and dependent on their own mothers." Clinicians believe, too, that many mothers of incest victims have knowledge of and acquiesce in the incestuous relationship. Following are two examples taken from case reports of a New York child protection agency:

The daughter, when she was eight years old, told the mother that she was being molested by the father. The mother slapped her and called her a bad girl. The case was finally reported by the mother seven years later when the victim tried to commit suicide.

All four daughters complained to the mother that the father was manipulating their breasts and genitalia. The mother told them that they misunderstood their father, that he was merely trying to show affection. The case was reported by a relative when the oldest girl became pregnant by the father.

Why would a mother allow this type of behavior to continue once she knew about it, or why would she refuse to accept knowledge of it when informed by her children or others? Most of those who study this area agree that mothers who are strong and healthy and competent individuals do not tolerate incest. But mothers who are powerless within their family structure, for any of several reasons, often tolerate many forms of abuse including incest. A 1979 study by David Finkelhor, a leading expert in the area, showed that girls whose mothers were often ill (such illness was often a previously undiagnosed depression) were almost twice as likely than the average girl to be sexually abused as children. In addition, emotional alienation between mother and daughter also seemed to increase the risk of incest to the child.

Such women, who cannot face the possibility of independent survival—life without their husbands or boy-friends—or who do not wish to risk their anger within the home, will frequently capitulate and, in effect, sacrifice one or more of their children in order to avoid rocking the boat. They feel that their first and primary loyalty is to their husband not to their children. In making such a decision they are obviously protecting their own positions at the expense of the welfare of their children.

If this is true for women in natural family units, it is even more true for divorced women. The incidence of stepfather/stepdaughter incest is five times higher than for natural father/daughter incest.

An example of the collusive divorced mother is provided by this case from the National Center for the Prevention and Treatment of Child Abuse and Neglect in Denver:

> *"The victim reported that when her previously divorced mother took a new lover, she went home to visit and was surprised to find that the boyfriend was making advances to her just as her own father had while her parents were married. When she reported the incident to her mother, the mother again refused to believe her just as she had when she was a child. 'You're always making up stories. What are you talking about?' "*

Recently, the following story appeared in a Toronto newspaper:

> *"The mother and stepfather of two young girls have been jailed for sexually abusing the children during orgies in their home. Mr. Justice Holland, describing the circumstances as 'as bad a case as can be,' sentenced the stepfather, 33, a security guard, to seven years in prison. The mother, 37, a waitress who lived common-law with the man for nine years, was sentenced to two years less a day in reformatory. The sexual assaults occurred over a period of four years, beginning in 1980 when the girls were 10*

and 11. Holland said, the girls were emotionally destroyed and would probably never recover. To the girls' mother he said, 'It is hard for me to believe any circumstances could justify your callous disregard for your daughters.' "

Married women have many reasons for turning a blind eye to incest. Divorced women have even more. They are often lonely, insecure, and afraid that they will "lose this man too." Sometimes it is just easier to believe that their child is exaggerating rather than to accept the truth and face additional emotional upheavals themselves. Women like this are often incredibly dependent on a man, and being suddenly on their own in the world can be so frightening that they are willing to sacrifice or believe anything to return to that safe harbor which a relationship with a man seems to provide. In addition, a woman is not going to be thinking of child molestation when she meets that "nice" man to whom her friends introduced her at a party. Child molesters do not advertise. It is often only after a incident has occurred that the woman may become aware there is something wrong. It is her behavior then that becomes critical. Many women simply choose not to see what they do not wish to see.

In addition to this, some clinicians say that they frequently see stepfathers who they believe chose their wives because they already had teenage children from a previous marriage. Roger Wolfe indicates that, in cases like this, sexual interest in the wife soon evaporates because it is really the children who interested the stepfather in the first place.

Considering this evidence it may be wise to question the validity of custody practices for female children in particular. Sometimes mothers may not make the best parents because they themselves may be either too weak or too dependent on a man to really protect the best interests of their children.

THE OTHER SIDE OF THE MYTH

One of the last great myths about divorce is that it is inherited: A mother who was herself a child of divorce gets divorced and then so will her children, down through the generations until family structure as we know it collapses completely. Such is not the case. Rather, it seems that the reverse is true.

As was said before, children of divorce are very resilient. They are not the emotionally scarred, wretched creatures they have been painted to be. While their own childhoods may not have been especially happy ones, they survived their parents' divorce, grew up, married, and perhaps divorced themselves. But as parents themselves they carried a wealth of experience with them into the divorce process. They had learned from their own parents' behavior, and for most of them there was no way they would repeat it in the case of their own children:

> *"Since I was a child of divorce, it's greatly influenced how I dealt with my daughters when I got divorced from their father. I tried not to let them spend too much time dwelling on the split. I did not put down their father in front of them nor was I prepared to prevent them from seeing him. I absolutely refused to behave the way my mother did or how I have seen too many friends behave with their children in a divorce situation."*

Chapter Five

The Daddy Dilemma

A father is a banker provided by nature.

French proverb

Sixty percent of divorced people have children under the age of eighteen. In 90 percent of the cases, those children are in the custody of their mothers *only:* Only the mother has a legal right to say what happens to the children, including shaping their relationship with their father by deciding when, where, and how often they should see him. The mother can legally remove the children to another state or another country, and she has a complete say in their educational, religious, and social environment. These rights are often granted to the mother without the consent of the father or of the children. In the modern divorce process, they are inalienable.

So severe is our attitude toward father custody that only 1.9 percent of all children under eighteen live in father-only households. This is less than the number of children living with strangers or other relatives (3.1 percent). Apparently we prefer just about any alternative to father custody. In fact, a father's only responsibility to his children after a divorce is to open his wallet or checkbook as often as is legally required. When it comes to parenting, fathers are expected to stay on the outside looking in and leave the important task of raising their children to the women to whom they were once married.

On the one hand, we take away the father's legal right to have anything to say about what happens to his offspring by awarding sole custody to the mother. On the other hand, we berate him for being an uninterested parent. We ask fathers to support completely children they see perhaps rarely, and when they are permitted a custody visit, we expect them to maintain a normal father-child relationship in a totally artificial environment.

How can fathers relate to their children in the easy, natural manner they did when they were part of each other's daily lives, if days or weeks separate their seeing each other? When they are together, one is often trying to find something to do and the other is trying to pretend he or she wants to do it. How many times can you or do you want to go to the zoo? How can you expect a natural flow in the relationship between parent and child when that relationship is restricted to a few hours on a weekend or is fit neatly into two weeks during summer vacation? You can't. It is unrealistic to expect either the father or the child to pull an intact relationship out of a hat every second Sunday of the month just because the court has said that that is their day to play father and child.

We have reached a point in our archaic divorce system where daddies are expected to live in exile from their families and still maintain their daddyhood. Impossible. Like a king without a country, a father without his children soon forgets what it feels like to be a daddy. Worse still, these children forget what it is like to *have* a father. This is one of the main ways that children of divorce lose out in our society. Not only do their parents divorce each other but their fathers are forced to divorce the children too. Yet our social and legal systems continue to support this procedure for restructuring divorced families as being in the best interests of the children. Why? What is so bad about fathers anyway?

MOMMY "MAVINS" AND DADDY "BANKERS"

Once upon a time, before the dawn of this century, children were seen as belonging to their fathers, first, foremost, and always. Paternal dominance over the children of the family was looked upon as not only right but "natural." Children were an asset to a man's estate. They had some commercial value.

With the increasing role segregation between men and women brought on by the industrial revolution, children were more and more frequently left solely to their mother's care, and women began to exert more influence over them. In England in 1839, the first blow to father-power was struck when the Talford Act eroded the father's right to absolute custody of his children by permitting awards to mothers of children under the age of seven. Since laws in the United States tended to follow precedent-setting decisions in English common law, the "tender years" doctrine was incorporated into our system of divorce and survives even today in cases where there are young children involved. The possibility of father custody in the case of young children remains extremely rare.

At the turn of this century, when psychologists and educators began to look seriously at the effects of divorce on the children involved, the "best interests of the child" doctrine became the major consideration when it came to plac-

ing children with one parent or the other. Since mothers
were thought to be obviously more maternal, more nurturing, more available, and more all-round suited to the role of
being a parent, then to the mothers went the children.

One would have thought that what seemed appropriate
in 1900 should look a bit out-of-date when perceived in light
of today's attitudes about family life and the roles of men
and women in general. We are supposedly not so anxious to
pigeonhole people according to their sex these days. Nevertheless men are even now generally perceived as being quite
unnecessary when it comes to the raising of children, if not
totally incompetent. Fathers have become a subgroup of
drones in our society, required only for the part they play in
conception. The courts and the majority of women still subscribe to the belief that not only is mother the best parent for
the child of the marriage, she is by far and away the *only*
possible choice for a parent after the divorce. Mommy
"Mavins" raise the children and Daddy "Bankers" under-
write their effort but are not supposed to interfere with their
maternal expertise.

This is true of parents whether they are married or divorced, but especially if they are divorced. This case of the
Mommy "Mavin" and the Daddy "Banker" is all too representative of the attitudes we hold about current parenting
roles. Men are the helpless incompetents who supposedly
can't open a jar of baby food while women are the experts
who know the mysteries of childhood and mothering instinc-
tively. And of course since the courts reflect the attitudes of
the rest of the society, then who else would get custody but
the mother? Certainly not dear old incompetent, irresponsible Dad.

But is it not amazing in a time when men are rushing
into delivery rooms all over the country to help their wives
give birth and to be part of their child's life from the first
moment it comes into the world, that if the couple should

divorce, five or ten years down the road, we then turn our backs on these men and say, "Sorry, pal, but the mother is the *real* parent. She gets custody and you get every other Sunday to play Daddy—but only as long as you keep up the payments"? How can we take a man who has spent the last several years of his life trying to be a parent in a way his own father would never have dreamed of and suddenly tell him that, by being part of a divorce, he is disqualified from being one?

THE "DELINQUENT DADDY" AND THE "DESERTED CHILD"

In July 1984, sheriff's deputies in Prince Georges County, Maryland, raided the homes of eighty-six people, only five of them women, and arrested them for alleged nonpayment of child support. In the middle of the night they dragged these people from their homes! Now I would never argue that the courts have no obligation to deal with a truly delinquent father, but under the present system a father who misses the twelfth payment of the year is considered delinquent even though he has made clear his desire to be a responsible parent for the majority of the year by paying the eleven payments before it. A father who is out of work, ill, or for some other reason incapable of paying the amount levied by a judge out of touch with current financial realities loses his personal rights and freedoms before he gets a chance to explain or challenge the situation. In another time we would have called this witch-hunting, but now we have somehow convinced ourselves that what we are doing is right and necessary. We read statistics that tell us that only 47 percent of ex-wives got the full amount of child support owed them, and we get angry. We do not read the figures that tell us that of the over 4 million women who were due child support in

1981, almost 3 million received support (72 percent). Or to put it another way, in 1983, of the 9 billion dollars due in child support 6.1 billion dollars were paid. We prefer instead to refer only to the 28 percent who did not receive support and lump all fathers into the category of deadbeats and delinquents. The breakdown according to racial origin for percentage of child support *paid* in *Statistical Abstract of the United States,* 1984, is as follows:

White	72.5%
Black	67.0%
Hispanic	65.9%

In order to justify our tawdry treatment of divorced fathers (to avoid sounding like something that might otherwise smack a little too loudly of simple revenge), we have invented a new role for the soon-to-be ex-father to play. His new title glares at him from the headlines on a daily basis. For now, he has been assigned the role of "Delinquent Daddy" (also known as "Deadbeat Daddy" and "Faithless Father"). Even if he tries to make his payments on time and sometimes gives more than is asked for, he knows that most people see him as that selfish, irresponsible lout who left "those wonderful children" and "that fine woman." Because opinions have a way of turning into realities, after a while he may come to see himself that way too, and then he adds another heaping tablespoonful of guilt to the crow he is expected to eat whenever he goes to pick up those children he used to refer to as *his* kids but who lately are beginning to look suspiciously like just *her* kids.

"Delinquent Daddy" is a very familiar figure in the media these days, and every divorced man with children has to face the flack that comes from his high visibility. Unfortunately, the majority of concerned and responsible divorced fathers have to suffer from the bad image generated by the few who deserve the bad press. But then these few were probably not very responsible fathers while they were married, and the fact that they got divorced did not suddenly create their unparentlike behavior; it merely removed it from inside the marriage to ouside the marriage.

In the research for this book, it became apparent that for the majority of divorced fathers the "Delinquent Daddy" label is incorrectly applied. In fact, when it came to the frequency with which the children saw their fathers, it was quite high:

Weekly	54%
Monthly	23%
Yearly	10%
Never again after divorce	13%

In some cases, the yearly visits were of long duration, such as a summer vacation, dictated by the geographical distance between father and child. In 60 percent of the cases where the child never saw the father again, the mother removed the child from the state or country where the father resided. Often she left no forwarding address.

"Every Sunday he had us over for dinner. We didn't stay long though because my older sister, the driver, didn't like Dad. After a bad year with my mother, I moved to his house and finished high school."

"After they were finally divorced I would spend the summers with my mother and the school term with my father."

"I saw him twice a week for two years and then my mother took me to another state and I saw him every summer."

"After the divorce, I never saw my father again. I don't think my mother wanted anything more to do with him and we lived in a different state."

It is true that as time passed, 63 percent of the children said they saw less of their fathers, 16 percent said they spent about the same amount of time with them, and 21 percent said they saw more of them. For those who reported seeing less of their fathers, it should not be assumed that this was necessarily the choice of the father. Rather, many of the children admitted that as they grew into their teenage years they developed friends and attachments outside the parental ones and would have seen less of their fathers and mothers even if the divorce had not occurred. In other cases respondents grew up, moved away or got married, and naturally enough spent less time with their parents, custodial or otherwise:

"After a while I got more involved with my friends and I didn't spend as much time with my dad as I used to."

"Once I moved away to college I didn't come home that often and so I didn't see much of either of my parents. I had my life to lead and they had theirs."

"The truth of the matter was I used to get so bored that I started to go round there less and less."

"Oddly enough I saw more of my father after I got married. He used to like to come over and play with his grandson."

It appears then that rather than giving up their role as father, most of these men tried to keep the relationship with their children going.

A favorite way of proving the far-flung existence of the "Delinquent Daddy" is to refer frequently to the popular, if ill-conceived story, of the struggling middle-aged woman and her four or five children who were deserted by "that man" who ran off and married a younger woman—*the rat*—and thereafter lost interest in his children. In fact, women in the forty-plus age group received 75 percent of the payments due them in 1981, while women in the eighteen to twenty-nine age group received only 62 percent. Older fathers, it seems, are more responsible, not less.

While it is true that four out of five men remarry and that they do it fairly soon (about two and a half years after the divorce), most of them do not leave for another woman. They may have in mind that they would like to have another relationship with a woman, but this is not the same thing. Responsible male parents do not suddenly turn into irresponsible parents just because they get divorced. Most men agonize over their relationships with their children and vice versa. A recent study by Pauline Boss at the University of Minnesota showed that it is fathers more than mothers who experience the most stress over the so-called empty nest syndrome. The study concluded that when a child goes away to college it is the fathers who were "significantly more preoccupied with the child's departure and thought a lot about the child" and were "more likely to have psychosomatic health problems such as anxiety, insomnia and an increase in smoking and drinking." The study also concluded that mothers may have lower stress when their children leave for college because they talk more about the child or "it may be that mothers are actually glad the kids have left home because it means less work for them." But, because it is usually the man who physically leaves once a marriage has broken down, we lay the blame for the end of the marriage firmly on his doorstep and punish him by depriving him of his children, the theory being that if he was so rotten as to leave "that fine woman," then how could he possibly be any good as a father?

In this study, the children said that 63 percent of the fathers were the ones who officially left the home. However, this did not necessarily mean they were deserting spouses. What it usually meant was that the father was being the "good guy" and letting his wife and their children remain in the comfortable, familiar surroundings of the family home. The children reported that 68 percent of their parents continued to see each other, 34 percent on good terms and the other 34 percent because of matters relating to finances or the children:

> *"My parents talked it over and decided that we should stay with Mom in the house and Dad would get an apartment nearby."*

> *"Since Mom was the one to leave, we stayed with Dad in the house but she would still come over and cook sometimes."*

> *"They both decided it wouldn't be fair for one of them to keep the house so they sold it and split the proceeds."*

But, our society still prefers to believe that *he* left *them*. It is interesting to note that in the 30 percent of the cases where it was the mother who left (either with or without the children), her departure did not detract from her credibility as either a parent or a spouse, and she invariably received custody if she wanted it as well as the family home.

Further light on the relationship between the so-called "Delinquent Daddy" and the "Deserted Child" was thrown by what the children did on their custody visits and how they perceived their relationship with their separated parent (usually their father) as changing as a result of the divorce. Forty-nine percent said that the time they spent with their separated parent was *better* after the divorce than before. Twenty-six percent said it was no different. Twelve percent said the relationship got worse. It seems that as far as the majority of the children were concerned, the fathers were not only not being delinquent, they were trying to be even better parents than before the divorce. Or perhaps the sudden release of tension brought about by ending the marriage had freed the fathers of some of their previous stress and they were now able to relate more openly to their children:

"After the divorce we used to spend time alone with Dad for the first time in our lives. He liked to go fishing so we would go fishing with him, something we never did while they were married because Mom didn't like that kind of thing."

"We just used to sit around and talk and then eat dinner. I think that's how I got to know my dad as a person, not just a father."

"He used to try so hard in the beginning trying to think up new places to take us. It took him a while to realize that we just wanted to see him and that we didn't always have to go somewhere."

"I used to go over to his new place and play with the baby he had with my stepmother. It was neat."

The majority of time on these custody visits was spent eating, usually in a restaurant if the father was single, but other activities similiar to those enjoyed before the divorce included going to the movies, the park, or the beach, skiing, camping, taking trips, visiting friends, and—interestingly enough—talking and shopping. Many of the children who had had no time or motivation to talk seriously with their fathers before the divorce found this activity particularly satisfying. The female children also noted an increase in their fathers' willingness to go shopping. Many felt that this urge to buy things for the child was one of the father's ways of trying to show his affection and that it was due to an awkwardness in how to spend enjoyable time with a teenage girl rather than a desire to buy their love. A few children noted that their fathers were really at a loss as to how to spend the time after a while or in the early stages of the new relationship:

> "I felt very uncomfortable with him in the beginning. I never really liked him that much while they were married and now I was thrown together with him every weekend. I don't think either one of us liked it too much—that forced closeness."

> "Every Saturday my father had custody of the three of us. I don't think he really had any idea what to do with us. Men didn't look after children in his ethnic background. He would pick us up and we would go to his favorite bar. He would meet with three or four other 'divorced fathers' who were friends of his and they would bring their kids too and watch the ball game on TV. We kids had a riot playing video games and eating junk food. My mother would have been furious if she had found out, but she never did. When I think about it now I realize that it may not have been the most wholesome atmosphere (though we kids thought it exciting), but my father needed the moral support of his friends and I think it helped him not to be alone. It wasn't so very different from my mother having her girlfriends over for coffee while they all baby sat their kids. But I guess people don't expect fathers to do that sort of thing."

THE CUSTODY WARS

Mothers are not good losers. But it seems from the evidence of this study that they are not good winners either. One would expect that when 90 percent of them have custody (85 percent in the case of this study) that that would be the end of it. Perhaps it is naïve to expect that the winner would graciously dole out to the loser his legally apportioned units of time with *her* children and let well enough alone. But such is not the case. Apparently mothers don't just want custody, they want complete custody and mind control as well.

Forty-two percent of the respondents said that their mothers tried to prevent them from seeing their fathers after the divorce, whereas only 16 percent of the custodial fathers tried to prevent them from seeing their mothers. The following are two examples of the lengths that some mothers are willing to go to to prevent fathers from seeing their children:

> *In 1984, a series of articles in the* Buffalo News *detailed the efforts of a woman to prevent her husband from seeing their three children on the grounds that he had been sexually abusing them. The divorce took place in 1979 and the battle is still going on in court.*
>
> *The courts found no legal evidence to support the accusation of sexual abuse, and the Erie County Grand Jury cleared the father of felony and misdemeanor sex-abuse charges raised by his ex-wife. The judge accused the mother of raising charges to deny the father his visitation rights. The mother was sentenced to six months in jail for refusing to allow her children to see their father. She was, however, released the following day. The children were then given back into her custody.*

Cases like this are not just isolated incidents as the following letter from a divorced father in Maine will show. Some people throw common sense to the wind when they get divorced and will stop at nothing, not even their children's welfare, to vent their wrath:

> *"I am going back to court this month to have a contempt trial with my ex-wife. I have not had my visitation with my two*

*minor children in one year now, and I have no guarantee that this
court date won't be just one more continuance (I have been in
court seven times waiting for action in the past year). I am finding out first hand that the courts go for the rights of the mother
vs. the father. I have been through a living nightmare, including
rape and death threats (my second wife and I are also going for
joint custody). My ex-wife has also brought me up on five felony
complaints, including threats to kill her and the kids, in an attempt to keep me from seeing them. Needless to say I have been
acquitted five times."*

It seems the father has few rights when it comes to his children, no matter what sort of behavior is exhibited by the
mother or how negative her influence may be over them.

In addition to attempts to prevent visitation, 54 percent
of the children said their mothers spoke badly of their fathers
in front of them:

*"She said he was selfish and lazy, that he had no ambition. She
took every opportunity to run him down."*

*"Dad never really said anything about Mom. But she used to say
a lot of nasty things to us about him. I think she was trying to
work out her anger toward him."*

*"After a while I stopped listening. You have to try and keep
things in perspective after all."*

*"She doesn't do it any more, but when I was young she would say
terrible things about him. All the bad, never the good. I always
felt that no one is all bad, but maybe if he was, then so was I."*

*"My mother was always talking about her sex life with my
daddy and saying how he was a lousy lover."*

*"Mother was always foul-mouthing him. She called him a
'cheating rotten S.O.B.' and a 'bastard.' Dad never said a*

word about her until years later when we could look back and discuss it."

"They both denigrated each other."

"Neither one of them ever said a word. Now that I am married and divorced myself, I often wonder what they thought of each other."

"I remember that Dad criticized Mom's boyfriend, and he said that she wasn't feeding us well enough (she wasn't). She told him to mind his own business."

Only 12 percent said their fathers spoke badly of their mothers, 24 percent said both parents spoke badly of each other, and 10 percent said their parents said nothing derogatory about the absent partner.

Interestingly enough, all these negative opinions did not sway the children in the direction intended, though it did have an effect on how they felt about the absentee parent. Fifty-one percent said that their custodial parent's negative attitude did not affect their own attitude and 49 percent said it did. But, of that 49 percent, 76 percent said that rather than causing them to have a negative opinion of their father, their mother's denigration of him produced a compensatory positive attitude in his defense. Some even said that their mother's constant griping caused them to put their father on a pedestal that was equally undeserved.

"I was brainwashed to think that my dad was crazy."

"Her attitude made me feel that I always had to come to my dad's rescue."

"Because my mother was so down on my father I think it may have strengthened my feelings for him."

"At first I reacted with anger and bitterness toward my dad, but later I realized what she was trying to do."

"I think it drew me closer to him. I felt a need to protect him."

"It affected my feelings for him in a positive way. I did not perceive my father as being 'bad,' as was so often said, but completely the reverse."

In spite of the fact that 54 percent of the mothers spoke badly of the fathers, only 16 percent of the respondents blamed their father for the divorce. Twenty-six percent blamed their mother, 18 percent blamed both, and 40 percent laid no blame at all.

"No one was to blame. They married too young and grew apart. It was just something that happened."

"I don't know how he managed to live with her as long as he did."

"I blamed him for not wanting to try harder to make the marriage work."

"I blamed my mother. She was always looking for something better and thought Dad just wasn't good enough for her I guess."

THE CUSTODY CONFIGURATION

The laws of custody have not changed much in the last eighty years. For instance 84 percent of the children in this study said all the children went to one parent. There was no consideration for the fact that in several cases some children wanted to be with one parent and some with another. When the children were in their later teens, however, they moved freely from the parent to whom custody had been awarded to the one they wanted to be with, and this is how most fathers in this study gained custody. It appears that the legal system places more importance on the relationship between brothers and sisters than on that between parents, especially fathers, and their children:

> *"My sister was definitely my mother's daughter as much as I was my father's. It would have made more sense if we could have each gone to the parent we wanted to be with instead of both of us going to my mother."*

Eighty-six percent of the children said they had no say at all in which parent got custody, even though some of them had a very definite opinion and preferred one parent to the other. For instance, 46 percent said they felt closer to their mother, but 39 percent said they felt closer to their father. This was not usually taken into account at the time of the custody decision.

The fact that so many children said that they were closer to their father indicates that in spite of the divorce, father and child managed to maintain a good feeling about their relationship. This is backed up by the fact that 41 percent of the children said they thought they were most like their father. In order to make this judgement they must have had some long-term knowledge of this parent as well as having a positive feeling about him. Only 27 percent said they felt they were more like their mother, and 33 percent said they felt that they were a little like both parents. Perhaps observing the mother's behavior during the divorce process caused the children, especially the female children, not to want to acknowledge a likeness with the mother. When asked if either parent's reaction to the divorce made them uncomfortable, 86 percent of those who said "yes" indicated that their mother's behavior made them feel that way.

Interestingly enough, it is usually the mother alone who breaks the news of the divorce to the child. In 52 percent of the cases mothers were the ones to do the telling, in 19 percent it was only the father, in 12 percent both parents did the job, and in 17 percent it was left to someone outside the immediate family such as a grandparent or friend to tell the children. It would appear that in order for the children to get a true picture of what is going on it is better if *both* parents sit down with the children, thereby avoiding any side-taking or blame-laying right from the beginning.

THE CUSTODY CONCLUSION

Most people think that parents want custody of their children because they love them and want to parent them enough to be willing to experience the hardships of single parenthood. This is a romantic illusion. We asked the question, "Why do you think your custodial parent wanted custody?" because it was thought that the children might be more likely to perceive the real machinations and motives of the divorce process from their position inside the marriage and perhaps present a more objective answer to this question than could be expected from an adult.

The following answers indicate that the children not only perceived the motive for wanting custody, but accepted it for what it was.

> *"I knew that my mother would never let my father have custody. She loved us kids. We were her whole life."*

> *"My mother was very maternal and she loved us."*

"I think she was afraid NOT to ask for custody because then people would think she wasn't a good mother or a nice person."

"In those days the kids went to the mothers. That's just the way it was."

"I don't think she really cared one way or the other, but she knew it would hurt my dad if she got sole custody so she went for it."

"It was best for everybody. Dad was away on business a lot so mother was the natural choice."

"She was afraid of what her mother would say if she didn't take us."

"Dad got custody because Mom was in an institution and couldn't take care of herself, let alone us."

Here is a tabulation of the reasons as perceived by the children:

Because custodial parent loved them	26%
A practical decision based on what was best for everybody	20%
Because of tradition	19%
To hurt the other parent	14%
For selfish reasons (e.g., the desire not to be alone)	12%
Fear of what people would think otherwise	9%

Though the love motive may have made up the single largest category and the "best interests" category came in second, 54 percent said their custodial parent wanted them for reasons that were basically not related to "what is best for the children" or parental love. This should help us reassess our current procedures. It is not enough to look at the parent who professes to want the child. One must also consider the motive of this person in order to determine what is truly in the best interest of the children.

WHY FATHERS ARE SO IMPORTANT

It is evident that divorced fathers don't have a lot of rights when it comes to their children. As one father said recently, "Now that she's remarried she would just like me to disappear and not see the kids at all, and I'm afraid that if I take her to court I'll lose them completely." But what about the children's rights to have a relationship with their fathers?

We are so wrapped up in the motherhood myth that for the most part we fail to see that fathers have any significance at all, aside from financial obligations. Yet several recent studies have shown that far from being negligible, the input of a father into his child's life is not only highly significant but essential for the well-being of the child and of the adult he will become.

In a study done by Dr. Mary Lund, a research fellow at the Child Care and Development Group at Cambridge University, it was discovered that "Divorce Orphans" who no longer see their fathers have greater emotional problems than other children of divorce. Self-esteem was lowest and emotional problems greatest in this group of children of divorce who, instead of blaming their fathers for leaving (as we have seen in this study), tended to turn their anger in on themselves. One out of three children was in this predicament. Lund concludes that some fathers are pushed out and others are convinced that not seeing their children is best for the children, but that the loss of their father is not beneficial to the children. "While a clean break may be precisely what the adults want, a break with one parent is not what most children need, nor is it to their benefit in most cases." As an answer to this situation, Lund recommends shared custody so that estranged fathers may participate fully in rearing their children.

Another study, done at Kent State University, found that boys more than girls needed the presence of their fathers especially as they approach the teenage years. "Girls have the same sex parent with them. Boys do not. As they move toward puberty, the need for the same sex parent increases." The author believes that the results of this study support the idea that boys should be placed more often with their fathers or in a shared custody situation.

But in a recent study conducted by Los Angeles psychologist Holly Barrett and author Elyce Wakerman, it was found that women who lost contact with their fathers in childhood through death or divorce had more marital problems and saw themselves as less ambitious and successful than women who had contact with their fathers. Among those who lost contact with their fathers because of divorce, 38 percent reported major marital problems. Perhaps this is because sex role stereotyping is not just acquired from the same sex parent (in this case the mother) but also from observing the interaction of the same sex parent with the opposite sex parent. Another recent study, made at the University of California at Irvine, revealed that the way a husband relates to his wife can affect his daughter's mental development and that the stronger the attachment between father and daughter, the better the daughter's social adjustment and later academic success.

We have perhaps underestimated the importance of fathers to daughters. In this survey it was the daughters, more than the sons, who missed their fathers the most after the divorce:

"I missed my father for years and felt disloyal for doing so. I think in many ways my situation was worse than usual because I was not allowed to talk about him or ask questions about him, so of course I spent a lot of time thinking about him and fantasizing what he would be like."

"I missed him very much, and it was never the same just seeing him weekends."

"At first I missed him terribly, but as time passed it seemed more normal for him not to be around so much. You adjust after all."

"I missed him terribly. When we would say goodbye after dinner or whatever I remember lingering in the truck or the car. I'd hug him and I often cried."

We cannot ignore that fathers are parents too. They want their children as much as mothers do, and it is unfair not to recognize this bond between fathers and children as much for the sake of the fathers as for the children who need them in different but equally special ways.

Chapter Six

The Divorce Equation

The biggest sin is sitting on your ass.

Florence Kennedy

*My eldest daughter came home from school last week and said:
"I'm glad you have a job, Mom. We've all been talking about it
at school, and all the ones whose mothers don't go out to work
wish they would, because they say it's a responsibility having
stay-at-home mothers who keep getting depressed and saying
their nerves are bad."*

Lynda Lee Potter

In centuries past children had a definite economic value for
their fathers. Now they have a very definite economic value
for their divorced mothers. If there is one rule when it comes
to divorce in the eighties, it is this: The parent who gets the
kids gets the cash—plus the house, the furniture, the car, the
insurance, and the dog—especially if that parent is the
mother. (Since I began this chapter, two different divorced
mothers have confessed to me that when they knew their
marriage was on the skids, they purposely got pregnant so as
to ensure maximum child support and maintenance for
themselves.) It seems that we have managed to evolve a system of divorce in which financial parity is no longer a possibility. It all hinges on custody.

There are two principles supporting the equation we
generally use to determine who gets the spoils in the divorce.

The first is that sole custody of the children should go to the mother. The merits of this train of thought have already been discussed. The second is that *because* she has the children she should therefore not be required or expected to work in order to support them. This demonstrates a very convoluted way of thinking. In the first place, because she has the children she needs more money than she would if she were single. But since we have taught entire generations of women to be financially dependent and not to look after themselves by getting a job, the divorced woman is then caught in a conundrum. Where will she get the money to support the children that she asked to have custody of? She can try and get support from the husband, and if this should fail, then there is always the federal, state, or local government. Or she could get a job.

The attitude that support for single women with children is a right and not a privilege has not always been the case. Just over forty years ago divorce for many women meant that they had to work if they expected to survive. But, as the following statistics will show, over the last four and one-half decades things have changed considerably for divorced women:

Percent of Women in the Labor Force		
	Single	Married (with husband present)	Divorced
1940	48.1%	14.7%	32.0%
1960	44.1	30.5	37.1
1970	53.0	40.8	36.2
1980	62.2	51.2	42.1

Though the participation rate for women in the work force has increased overall from 27.4 percent in 1940 to 52.1 percent in 1982, the separate groups listed above have not increased at the same rate. In 1940 the ratio of divorced women working compared to married women was more than two to one, but over the decades this ratio has been gradually eroded. In 1968 more married women were recorded in the labor force than divorced women (38.3 percent to 35.8 percent) for the first time. Now there are 1.21 married women working for each divorced woman who works. In addition, the unemployment rate for divorced women with children is higher than for married women with children. In 1982, the unemployment rate for married women overall was 7.1 percent (10.1 percent for those with children under six), for separated women it was 14.5 percent (20.1 percent for those with children under six), and for divorced women, 8.9 percent (13.5 percent for those with children under six).

Over the last fifteen years, as divorce settlements have turned in favor of women more and more, we have seen fewer and fewer divorced women in the work force. Relative to other groups of women their need to be self-supporting has been curtailed if not eliminated. This is primarily because of our attitudes toward mothers and custody. It appears, therefore, that the women who logically would need the income from working outside the home the most are the ones who participate in the labor force the least.

WHY WORK IS A FOUR-LETTER WORD

How then do divorced mothers live? The answer is quite simple: We support them, either directly with maintenance or welfare, or through child support and related divorce settlement assets or from government assistance programs such as the Aid to Families with Dependent Children program. This program, though financed equally by federal and state funds, is run by the states. To be eligible for A.F.D.C. payments a woman must be pregnant or have at least one child, she must live with and take care of the child, and the husband or father of the child must be either unwilling or unable to support the child. This means that the father of the child must be dead, disabled, or not living with the mother. Of course, since all fathers are required to support their children, the welfare department is entitled to sue the father to recover the support it has provided to the family under this program. And that is no small sum.

In 1982, 13 billion dollars were spent on support in the form of A.F.D.C. payments. Forty-five percent of those payments went to divorced or separated mothers with children. Many people would use this figure to give credence to what has been called the "feminization of poverty" and at the same time do a little "Daddy Bashing" on the side. While it is true that there are currently 3.6 million female-headed poor families—up 82 percent since 1960—it is also true that, while the poverty of many of these families stems initially from divorce or separation, they continue to remain in poverty for other reasons. One reason is that we make no demands upon them to improve their situation. Because they are mothers, we make it possible for them to be mothers and do nothing else.

As Senator Edward Kennedy pointed out in 1978: "We will give you an apartment, and furniture to fill it. We will give you a TV set and a telephone. We will give you clothing and cheap food and free medical care and some spending money besides. And, in return you only have to do one thing: just go out and have a baby. And faced with such an offer it is no surprise that hundreds of thousands have been caught in that trap that our welfare system has become." According to Walter Williams, a professor at George Mason University, "Poor people may be poor but they are not stupid. If you make it easier for them to live without working many of them will, just as those in other income groups would."

If this is true of the poor in general, it is even more true of divorced women because they are encouraged to claim motherhood as an excuse for not participating fully in either their own support or that of their children.

What we have created is a "divorce ghetto" populated by women and their children on the one side and husbands and often their second families on the other side. The idea that a divorced woman and her children live in poverty while her ex-husband "lives it up" is a fantasy. In 50 percent of divorce cases, the standard of living is seen to decline, at least initially, for *all* concerned. In 20 percent of cases the standard of living of the divorced woman actually improves. But the decline in living standard is usually not the fault of people getting divorced. It is frequently the fault of the divorced woman's feeling that it is right and just for her not to work becaue she has custody of the children, thereby throwing the burden of supporting two households onto the other parent. If poverty among divorced women is such an issue, then why aren't more of them willing to seek some form of employment to better the lot of themselves and their children?

WHY WOMEN DON'T WORK

In female-headed households below the poverty level only 18 percent of the total said they worked full time (15.8 percent white and 22.3 percent black). The reasons given for not working are as follows:

Reasons for Not Working		
	White	Black
Keeping house	69.0%	54.0%
Illness	15.5	20.7
Unable to find work	7.9	17.5
In school	3.3	4.5

One has to wonder how so many women below the poverty level can find enough housework to do everyday to justify not working, unless they choose not to work. Most people will point out that raising children is a full-time job, which is why mothers should not be expected to go out and get a job. However, Dr. Sandra Scarr, in *Mother Care/Other Care*, points out that "employed mothers spend as much time as non-working women in direct interactions with their children." Dr. Scarr, herself a mother of four, cited large-scale research studies by Lois Hoffman, a social psychologist at the University of Michigan, who found that the average full-time mother spent less than ten minutes per day playing or reading with her preschool child. In contrast they spent an average of thirteen minutes eating with their children and twenty-one minutes watching television with them. Dr. Scarr went on to say, "There is no evidence that children do better if mother stays at home for the first three years of life, or for the first three months of life. In fact, the age of the child does not seem to be a factor at all." She also believes that in many cases children are better off in a stimulating day care environment than at home. However, although there is no great difference for the children, there certainly is for the mothers: "Mothers at home do have one great advantage over those who are employed: leisure," she said.

In a 1983 nation-wide study, based in Minneapolis, of

8,000 children and 10,000 parents, it was revealed that parents spend the same amount of time each day with their teenage children as they do watching the TV news. In fact, 44 percent of adolescents said they spend less than thirty minutes a day with their mothers.

Also, the notion that children of working mothers suffer in their development appears to be nothing more than just that, a notion. Psychologist Adele Eskeles Gottfried and Allen W. Gottfried of California State University reported in a recent study of children aged one to five years that 36 percent of the mothers worked when their children were one year old and 56 percent worked by the time their children were five. They discovered that the home environments of the children of working mothers were no less enriching and stimulating than homes where the mothers did not work. They also reported that the scores of the children of working mothers on six standard developmental tests were equivalent to the scores of children with stay-at-home mothers. They concluded that what was crucial to the children's development was the child's experiences, *not* the employment status of the mother.

If this is the case, then having children at home is not a good reason for divorced women not to work. A more likely reason for their not working is that they can find other avenues of support—their ex-husbands and the state.

Adding credibility to the argument that custody in many cases ensures a guaranteed income for divorced mothers that they are loath to surrender is the recent New York State decision about joint custody. In 1982 a bill making joint custody an option for divorced parents passed in the New York State legislature. It was vetoed twice by the governor under pressure from women's groups such as the New York State chapter of NOW and the National Center on Women and Family Law, who felt that joint custody would jeopardize a mother's financial stability (i.e., if mothers did not have sole custody of the children, then they would not be receiving the same amount in support payments as they had previously and might not expect to do as well when it came to dividing up the assets of the marriage). In addition, pressure from the New York Women's Bar Association, which also opposed the bill, means that future attempts to pass such legislation are unlikely to mandate the alternative of joint custody but merely to make it a possible option. According to Harriet N. Cohen, who holds the chair of the Matrimonial and Family Law Committee of the New York Women's Bar, the group is opposed to joint custody and to the presumption of joint custody because "it forces a woman to prove why sole custody might be more appropriate for *her* child and she ends up taking a *lesser financial settlement as a compromise.*" Money, it seems, is more of an issue than the best interests of the child for some women.

The final argument in favor of divorced mothers not working is: Who would look after the children if they did go to work? After all, married women can work because their husbands can help with the baby sitting. Except, as most married women know, that is not the way things are usually handled.

The argument against coddling custodial mothers for this reason is simple: 51 percent of white mothers and 58 percent of black mothers with preschool children work. For their favorite child-care options, see the table on page 101. If these women can work and have children, especially children who are very young, then why can't the same be expected of divorced mothers?

By making it easier for divorced women with children to get support, we are undermining their independence as people, as well as putting increased burdens on the state and on their ex-husbands. By encouraging them to believe that they should stay home and not work because they have children (even though it seems the majority of their time is not

Day Care Choices of Working Women*		
	with husband present	with husband absent
Care in another home	40.7%	38.2%
Group care	13.4	20.2

* If you pay for day care for a child under fifteen so you can work, there is a tax credit that may help with the cost. The credit offsets your taxes, dollar for dollar and, depending on your income, ranges from 20 to 30 percent up to $2,400 for the care of one child, up to $4,800 for two or more.

spent in mothering), we are also doing the children in their care a great disservice, by providing the children with a role model that says you can get something for nothing.

"DADDY, I NEED MY CHECK"

A recent National Urban League report on the 477,000 A.F.D.C. single-parent households, almost all of them headed by women, in Los Angeles concluded the following: "This is a prescription for disaster. A child growing up in such circumstances has two strikes against him or her from the start and may well grow into adult-hood as a member of a growing sector of our society perpetually without gainful employment or any hope of ever escaping the clutches of poverty."

There has been some discussion over the past few years about how much welfare dependency is passed on from one generation to the next. There is now a consensus of opinion that such long-term effects do exist. Economist Robert Lerman of Brandeis University noted that 70 percent of those who came from families on welfare neither attended school nor had a job. "The existence of another person in the family who works raises the chances that young people will stay in school or get a job." Lerman also indicated that there was a strong link between female-headed households and diminished opportunities for young people. His study was backed up by Sara McKanahan of the Institute of Research on Poverty who discovered that regardless of place of residence, parents' education, or race, young people who lived with single mothers were more likely to have dropped out of school than those living in two-parent households.

It is obvious that by encouraging divorced mothers to assume a role of dependence, whether on the state or on their ex-husbands, instead of one of self-sufficiency, we are also condemning the children in their care to a lifetime of the same, because they have no adequate role model to observe. If children do not see the parent with whom they spend most of their time engaged in gainful employment, but rather observe her to be the recipient of funds from some invisible or absent entity, then they are bound to have a warped opinion of how money is acquired. They may easily think that they, too, are entitled to a certain amount of money without working, thereby ensuring another generation of welfare recipients or nonworking divorced mothers.

For instance, a mother had her nine-year-old daughter call her father on the first of every month (even though he had never been late with his support payments) to say, "Daddy, I need my check." Even at that tender age she was learning a pattern of financial dependence on someone else. As a woman she would very probably grow up to perceive herself to be financially dependent on her husband, the way she had been taught to be dependent on her father. Would it not have been better if, instead of trying to make the father feel guilty about the divorce, the mother had concerned herself with showing her daughter the importance of self-sufficiency?

THE UNIFORM MARRIAGE AND DIVORCE ACT

One of the reasons that so many divorced women can afford not to work is that, in the last few years, the laws about divorce and the women involved in it have become extremely paternalistic. Though many women regard as a victory the way the courts now bend over backward to give them everything possible under the law—and, in fact, have even changed the law to accommodate their "special" status— they would be better advised to regard it as a defeat, because by being the recipients of this special treatment they are being denied the right to be treated as equals with men. The legal system is now being just as sexist about the woman's position as it was when women received nothing, not even custody, if a couple got divorced. Special status and equality do not go hand in hand. An example of this is the Uniform Marriage and Divorce Act.

In 1970 the National Conference of Commissioners on Uniform State Laws approved and recommended for enactment by all states the Uniform Marriage and Divorce Act. The act was drawn up with sections relating to property division, child support, economic maintenance for a "dependent spouse," child custody, and enforcement. Though many states have not yet adopted this act (largely because the only grounds for divorce is irretrievable breakdown of the marriage), the sections relating to support and custody are typical of the way the judiciary perceives the situation in most states.

In Section 307 (Disposition of Property), the act recommends that the court take into consideration "the economic circumstances of each spouse at the time the division of property is to become effective, including the desirability of awarding the family home or the right to live therein for reasonable periods to *the spouse having custody of any children.*"

Further on, in Section 308 (Maintenance) it says: "... the court may grant a maintenance order for either spouse only if it finds that the spouse seeking maintenance ... is unable to support himself through appropriate employment or *is the custodian of a child.*"

In Section 309 (Child Support) the act says: "... the court may order either or both parents owing a duty of support to a child of the marriage to pay an amount reasonable or necessary for his support after considering all relevant factors including: ... 2) *the financial resources of the custodial parent* and 3) the standard of living the child would have enjoyed had the marriage not been dissolved."

Here, then, we have all the factors leading to the divorce equation nicely outlined: (1) Whoever gets custody gets the house; (2) because they have custody they do not have to work and are entitled to receive maintenance to pay for their own upkeep and for the house; and (3) because they are not working and therefore have few if any financial resources, they are also entitled to child support. In addition, this support shall be an amount that enables the child to live at the level he or she lived at before the marriage broke down.

KIDS + CUSTODY = CASH

It is often pointed out that either the father or the mother may be charged with paying support, but in practice it is almost always the father.

THE HIDDEN COSTS OF CHILD SUPPORT

You may have heard a lot about child-support payments being so small as to be negligible in the grand expense of raising a child. But in the survey for *Solomon's Children,* 69 percent knew how much child support their mothers were receiving for them, and the average amount per child per month was $200.00.

The schedule below, from the state of California, is an example of the type used as a guideline when courts are deciding on support payments. (Remember, though, it is a guideline only. Courts are *not required* to follow it exactly.)

Schedule For Child Support Payments Where No Spousal Support Is Ordered			
Noncustodial Parent's Net Monthly Income	One Child	Two Children	Three or More Children
$ 400.00	$100.00	$100.00	$100.00
500.00	125.00	150.00	175.00
600.00	150.00	200.00	225.00
700.00	150.00	250.00	275.00
800.00	150.00	250.00	300.00
900.00	175.00	275.00	350.00
1,000.00	175.00	300.00	375.00
1,200.00	200.00	350.00	450.00
1,400.00	250.00	400.00	525.00
1,600.00	250.00	450.00	600.00
1,800.00	275.00	500.00	675.00
2,000.00	300.00	550.00	750.00
Above 2,000.00	Court's Discretion		

The problem with schedules such as this is that though they are useful for giving a general idea of what you can be expected to pay given your earnings, they are concerned more with what the paying parent earns than with what the children's needs may be. How else can you explain that three children cost $450 a month if you earn $1,200, two cost $350 and one costs $200 a month for the same salary? Surely, economies of scale do not apply to feeding and clothing children. Should you be asked to pay 25 percent of your income for three children if you earn only $400 a month, but 37.5 percent of your income for three children if you earn $2,000? Does this not punish the parent who earns more money by expecting him to pay a larger chunk proportionally of that salary just because he earns more? Does anybody take into consideration that as one's salary increases so does one's cost of acquiring that salary and that therefore a relatively higher net income does not necessarily mean a disposable income that has increased by the same amount?

It would seem from the above schedule that what a child costs is based on how much you earn and on how many siblings he has, not on how much or how little he actually needs. Would it not be better to determine a base figure of what it costs to feed, clothe, and house a child and proceed from there?

In addition to the legally required amount that is considered necessary to support a child (and which varies substantially from judge to judge), it was also discovered that child cost did not often equal the legally ordered amount of support. In 63 percent of the cases the parent paying the child support, usually the father, was also contributing the cost of extraordinary expenses such as going to camp, dental visits, college tuition, etc. While 52 percent of the respondents said that, to their knowledge, their support did not increase during the time they remained in the home, for those who did receive an increase, the amounts were usually substantial—from 80 to 400 dollars in one case for one child over a five-year period and from 100 to 400 dollars in another case. It would not be fair to assume that the father's income or the child's real expenses had risen proportionally during that time. In addition to these expenses fathers often find that additional charges are being levied against them for their child's support that did not exist before the divorce:

"All of a sudden he's taking violin lessons and riding lessons, which are very expensive. He never showed any inclination to do these things while I was married to his mother. It is not that I don't want him to have these things, it's just that I think his mother is behind all this somehow, trying to squeeze as much money from me as she possibly can."

"I don't understand why an eight-year-old girl has to go to the hairdresser twice a month and take skating and skiing lessons and go to the most expensive camp around. I couldn't afford it while we were married, but now that we are divorced I certainly can't afford all this in addition to the other payments I have to make."

"Part of our divorce settlement was that I should pay for him to go to Harvard. Not just a good college, but Harvard! No one in her family ever even went to college and, besides, he's only five. Who knows if he's got the brains to get in?"

WHAT DIVORCE DENIES THE CHILDREN

We asked the "children of divorce" if they thought they had been denied anything as a result of the divorce. This question was specifically included in the section on finances, but many chose to answer it another way. Only 14 percent said they had been denied things that only money could buy, while 36 percent said they had been denied nothing by their parent's divorce. But 50 percent said they had been denied on the emotional level; of these, 68 percent said they had been denied a father.

"The only thing I was denied was family togetherness. Dad gave us just about everything we could want or asked for. There was always lots of money at Christmas and birthdays."

"The only thing I was denied was a father."

"The divorce didn't make any difference that way. We were financially strapped before and we were financially strapped after."

"My mother got the house and all the property. Later when it was sold those who sided with her in the divorce were rewarded. Because I was living with my father I got nothing. He supported me until he was laid off from his job after twenty-two years. He went from an executive job to being a security guard just so he could support us kids. I got a job and moved out to help alleviate some of the burden."

"I was denied all the things my friends had like trips to Europe and nice clothes. I couldn't even have my own car."

"I know that I would have had more material things if they had stayed married but that doesn't mean I would have been any happier."

"I was denied a lot of material things. I wore hand-me-downs till I was on my own."

"I missed having a father the most. Father/daughter scouting events were hardest, I think."

VARYING SUPPORT ORDERS

What does the law say about terminating and changing child-support orders? According to Section 316 of the Uniform Marriage and Divorce Act: ". . . the provisions of any decree respecting maintenance or support may be modified only as to installments accruing subsequent to the motion for modification and only upon showing changed circumstances so substantial and continuing as to make the terms unconscionable."

In practice, it is generally very difficult for a father to reduce his support payments. In fact, many men who find themselves unemployed, laid off, or injured often find they cannot get their support payments reduced by the court, and so they simply take matters into their own hands and stop paying altogether. Once a father has demonstrated his ability to make payments at a certain level, even if his circumstances do change (such as the birth of a child in a second marriage), the court generally regards him as being responsible for continuing the payments at that previous level. As for stopping the payments permanently, Subsection C of the act says: "Unless otherwise agreed in writing or expressly provided in the decree, provisions for the support of a child are terminated by the emancipation of the child but not by the death of a parent obligated to support the child." In other words the burden of support then shifts to the father's estate, if any, even though he may have had other plans for it in his will.

Though many men think they will be free of the burden of child support when the child is eighteen, the fact is that as long as the child is dependent, even if he or she is technically an adult, the father can be expected to contribute to the child's support.

In a recent judgment from the Supreme Court of Ontario, a judge ordered a father to pay 900 dollars a month in support payments, 300 dollars of which was to be used to support his "two children," aged twenty and twenty-two, who still lived with his ex-wife. In a similar case two daughters aged twenty-two and twenty-three were given support even though were both living with their boyfriends away from the parental home. In a case in New Jersey, which followed a precedent-setting decision by the New Jersey Supreme Court where a father was ordered to continue paying "child support" to his adult child who wanted to remain in school, the New Jersey Tax Court decided that the children of a well-to-do doctor were entitled to both a private school education and a college education paid for by their father because the court found that considering the values and backgrounds of the parents they (or rather the father) had a legal duty to provide their minor and adult children an education related to their station in life. Some children it seems are taking a lesson from their mothers and looking to their fathers for support even though they are no longer children and are ostensibly capable of looking after themselves.

Although many people believe that the burden of support falls on the mother of custodial children (a rather difficult task considering so many of them do not work), this survey does not bear that out. In fact, 56 percent of Solomon's Children said their custodial parents did not contribute to their support, while 78 percent of the respondents said that they themselves contributed, on the average, 20 percent of the cost of their own support while living at home. This indicates that the bulk of the burden of raising a child to age eighteen was placed on the father and the child himself or herself, not the mother. In addition, 55 percent of the children said that they were aware that the custodial parent had been using the child-support money for reasons other than their support:

> *"My father set up a bank account for my mother to support us with, but she also used it to drink and smoke and buy clothes for herself."*

> *"My mother was an alcoholic and a lot of the child-support money went for that."*

"My mother ran around with a number of younger men and she used to spend some of the money on them."

"She liked to travel and so that's what she used it for."

"She spent it on clothes for herself and food for her horses."

"She didn't handle money very well and so had trouble passing it along to us."

"At one point we had to borrow money for food from a neighbor soon after my mother had bought a new set of china. I also know she spent some on clothes for herself."

"Dad said she wasn't spending the money on food, that was for sure, after he found out that we were having Hamburger Helper every night."

One of the things that angers fathers the most is that they pay the money every month but they have virtually no control over where it goes. Many end up shouldering additional expenses by buying clothes or extra items during custody visits that should have been paid for out of the support money. But ex-husbands have little or no recourse. They have to pay the full amount that is legally required and cannot deduct the cost of the additional items they themselves pay for. It is just expected that a mother will do what is best for *her* children with the money she gets from their father for their support, although that is not always the case.

Recently a man wrote to say that his oldest daughter, who lived with her mother in another state, had stopped speaking to him some months previously and had then dropped out of college. It took him some time to find out that she had dropped out because the money he had been sending to the mother for his daughter's expenses at school had not found its way to his daughter. Instead, the mother had kept the money for herself and had told both the daughter and the son that the father had ceased to make his support payments. The son got a job to pay room and board to his mother, who all the while was putting the support payments for both children in her own bank account. There was little the father could do except to pay the children their support money directly.

THE TRUST ALTERNATIVE

The trust fund is a possible answer to the oft asked question, "What happens to the money I pay?" In an attempt to ease his mind on where the child support money actually goes, a support-paying father might be interested in investigating the possibility of setting up a trust to handle his child-support payments.

There are two types of trusts: testamentary and living. The living trust, which applies in this case, is created during the lifetime of the person who sets it up. Actual details of a trust will vary according to the state it is set up in, because the laws that govern trusts vary from state to state. These laws are essentially concerned with setting limitations on the powers of the trustee and on the length of time the property will be held in trust. For instance, no state will allow a trust to operate indefinitely. Still, that is not the issue here. We are concerned with setting up a trust until the children are of age or until they finish their education, whichever is decided upon in the divorce decree as the term for support. You can set whatever conditions you want except for the limitations set forth in the laws of the particular state in which you set up the trust (you can set up a living trust in a state other than the one you live in if you like their laws better, as long as the trust has some material connection with the designated state, i.e., it could be the state where the trustee lives as opposed to the state where you live).

The one who creates the trust (settlor) can make his own rules as to how the trust is going to operate. For instance, the settlor—in this case the father—can designate the purpose of the trust (i.e., to pay child support); determine the amount of property it will contain; set the length of time it will last; pick the beneficiaries; direct how much they will receive and when; and he can further set conditions that the beneficiary must meet in order to receive the income. He can also provide alternate disposition in case his conditions aren't met.

In other words, a father setting up a trust to pay his child support might perhaps make payment dependent on a monthly or yearly accounting of what the money has been spent on, with proper receipts required, etc. If these are not forthcoming or are inaccurate, then he could have the money paid into court while a judge decides on whether the mother is using the support payments for the benefit of the intended children or not.

In order to maintain control of the trust and alter it or amend it as circumstances demand, the father would be wise to make the living trust revocable. This permits him to terminate the trust and take back the property if he wants to. It also gives him the right to change the terms of the trust, including the names of beneficiaries and the amounts and conditions under which they are to get their share.

Unfortunately, revocable trusts do not enjoy the tax advantages of other trusts. But they do allow the father some peace of mind when it comes to how his child-support money is being spent and on whom and by having the money managed by a third party, it also removes him personally from any harassment or aggravation he may be subject to.

FORCING THE SUPPORT SITUATION

In 1984 there was a lot of talk about "parents" not living up
to their responsibilities to pay child support. Health and
Human Services Secretary Margaret Heckler said, "It's time
for parents to take their responsibilities seriously, and the
law will give us the tools to make it happen." In Tallahassee,
Florida, Judge Charles McClure said, "I don't see how parents can justify not supporting the children they helped
bring into this world." Generally, it was a good election year
issue.

But what politicians and the media meant by "parents"
was fathers. Feminists had a lot to say about what we were
doing to women and children, and President Reagan cut
back A.F.D.C. payments, thereby forcing a lot of women off
state welfare and onto ex-husband welfare. So after *Paternity
Amnesty Week* failed (during which fathers who were late or
not paying had a chance to rectify the situation), the Maryland child-support raids came as no surprise. During this
whole time nobody said anything about it being a mother's
responsibility to support her children as well as a father's.

The eventual outcome of all this was a bill passed in the
late summer that required states to withhold wages when
"parents" failed to make court-ordered child-support payments after thirty days. Federal and state income tax refund
checks were also to be held back to cover overdue payments.
In addition, states were encouraged to co-operate with each
other in the handling of support cases that crossed state lines.
Fathers and their second families were up against the wall.
No matter what emergency might arise, the money for child
support was gone even before it came into the home whether
they could afford it or not. There was no arguing about the
amount, no excuse for being late, no one to listen to the other
side of the issue. Of course, a man could go to court if he felt
the money was being taken unfairly, but then it would be

awfully hard to get back money that had been spent by a woman who wasn't making any, and besides it would cost him money to go to court.

Men's groups across the country were up in arms. Many of them cited the fact that the ability to withhold child support was sometimes a father's only way of making sure he saw his children. "I understand why men who can't see their children refuse to pay," said Kenneth Pangborn of MEN International, a fathers' rights group that contends that a third of all support claims are exaggerated. "Not all fathers are devils," said family law expert Doris Freed. "Some fathers feel that the whole custody battle is unfair."

But fair or not, with the backing of women's groups, fathers' rights and the rights of their other dependents have been relegated to second place. Some women and children, it seems, are regarded as more equal than others under the current law.

Garnishment of salaries for support was not totally new. It is just that it had now moved into the private sector in a much larger way. Previously, most laws to force child-support payments had only been used as a very extreme measure.

For instance, the Tax Reduction and Simplification Act of 1977 amended Section 303(b) of the Consumer Credit Protection Act to restrict the amount of an individual's earnings that may be garnished for the support of any person (child support or alimony). Prior to this amendment there were no federal limitations on the amount of earnings that could be garnished for this purpose. Section 303(b) now provides that the maximum amount of an individual's disposable earnings that may be garnished for support are as follows:

1. Fifty percent is garnishable if the individual is already supporting his spouse or dependent

child and the garnishment for support concerns someone else (i.e., former spouse or other dependent children).

2. Sixty percent is garnishable if the individual is not supporting any such persons.

3. These percentages are increased to 55 percent and 65 percent respectively if the garnishment order concerns payments more than twelve weeks in arrears.

Perhaps three people can live on one-half of a man's income while two people live on the other, but it is doubtful. One has to wonder why a man's second family is supposed to be able to live on 10 percent of his salary, assuming he is permitted 40 percent for himself, but his first family gets a whopping 50 percent or 60 percent, depending on the circumstances. This may account for why 74 percent of the women (some with children) who are in a second marriage find they have to work.

It is not necessary that you be employed to have your income garnished for support. The Federal Employees Compensation Act of 1974 also provides that "disability compensation payments are, however, subject to garnishment for alimony and child support payments if the legal process is served in accordance with State Law...."

There is also provision made for the garnishment of the pay of military personnel for child-support enforcement, which follows the same 50 percent and 60 percent levels outlined above and which includes not only wages but bonuses, incentive pay or retirement pay as well as salary. So too the Veterans Administration can garnish payments made by it as compensation for a service-connected disability.

And now, employers in the private sector can also be expected to garnish their employees' salaries for being late with child-support payments. This is not supposed to affect the employer's attitude toward that employee, who cannot be dismissed by law because of a garnishment order. It is, however, unlikely that he will be promoted because of it, either. A recent case in California has the ex-wife suing the employer for firing the husband as a result of such an order, because she says that by firing him the employer is putting her child-support payments in jeopardy.

STEPPARENT SUPPORT

There has been some concern in the last few years on the part of stepparents who wonder just how much of the burden of support for their spouse's previous family they are expected to shoulder. This is particularly true in the case of women who marry men who have children from a previous marriage, because it is men who generally do most of the supporting.

Many a woman in a second marriage, who is employed, has found that after the wedding ceremony, and sometimes even before it, the court, at the behest of the ex-wife, is casting avaricious glances at her paycheck as well as at her husband's. In many cases the second wife will be asked to disclose her income to the court if there is an order to vary support so that the court can take that money into consideration when determining the increased amount of support. This is wrong. In some cases the second wife is supporting her own children from her first marriage, or is planning to use her income for children in a second marriage. The inequity arises particularly in cases where nonworking first wives think they are entitled to additional support for their children because their husband's second wife *is* working. The days when a woman's income was seen as her husband's property are apparently not yet over.

Some states are beginning to realize the unfairness of

the situation of stepparent support, though only in respect to the rights of the spouse of the *custodial parent* (i.e., the stepfather in most cases). California for example has a statute (Civil Code 5127.6) that makes a stepparent's income "available" for the support of his or her stepchildren. However, in 1983 the Court of Appeals restricted this law to situations where the custodial parent is on welfare. It has ruled that the income of the new husband or wife (of the custodial parent) is irrelevant in a proceeding brought about by the custodial spouse for increased child support, especially when a marital contract between the custodial spouse and his or her new spouse has specified that the income of the new spouse is separate property. But what about the new spouse of the *noncustodial* parent—the spouse of the one generally paying the support?

We have a long way to go before rectifying the inequities in the current system of child support that favor some parents over others and some children over others. One way to improve the situation immensely would be to encourage mothers to take on their share of the economic burden of raising a child, instead of expecting fathers and their new spouses to shoulder the entire burden.

NO MORE DADDY DEDUCTIONS

Child support is not tax deductable to the one who pays it or taxable to the one who receives it. This has long been a bone of contention with many fathers. Further, since 1985, as the final factor in the divorce equation, daddies who pay child support are no longer able to claim the child tax exemption either.

In the past the dependency exemption for a child went to the parent providing more than 50 percent of the support—usually the father, as we have seen. But now it goes to the custodial parent, unless that parent waives the right to claim the child as a deduction.

So mother now has custody, cash, and a tax deduction. Plus, she is still not expected to work to contribute to the child financially or to be accountable for how she spends the money she receives to support the child. The *new* divorce equation then looks like this:

KIDS + CUSTODY = CASH + TAX DEDUCTION − WORK − ACCOUNTABILITY

Chapter Seven

How Children Feel About Divorce

If life is to be sustained, hope must remain, even where confidence is wounded, trust impaired.

Erik Erikson

Life is like an onion: you peel it off one layer at a time and sometimes you weep.

Carl Sandburg

One of the primary biases against divorce in our society is the belief that in those divorces which involve children, dependent or otherwise, the occurrence of the divorce provides a permanent scarring of the young psyche, a trauma from which the children never recover. So intense is this belief that some researchers who study the effects of divorce have insisted that, as an event, divorce has a more severe effect on the outlook of the child than the death of a parent. This is difficult to believe given the responses to this survey.

FINDING OUT HOW CHILDREN FEEL

In the past, to find evidence of how serious the effects of divorce truly can be, we have gone right to the source and asked the children involved. When we heard that some of them were unhappy or had bad feelings about the event at the time, we held this up as proof that divorce was a truly terrible thing.

Very often, however, children have been asked how they felt or are feeling about their parents' divorce relatively close to the event, or they are asked by a psychologist or psychiatrist in an official setting because they have already sought therapy. In any event, it is unlikely that the many children who have adjusted well to their parents' divorce will receive the attentions of researchers.

It is true also that, even when they are very young, children realize that adults expect them to be upset by their parents' divorce, so they tell the adults what they want to hear. They tell about the bad feelings and perhaps try to conceal the good or indifferent feelings because, even to themselves, they may question their right to such feelings. Or if they are even slightly cunning they may see the whole situation as possibly being advantageous as long as they are giving off the correct distress signals.

In any event, it is very hard to tell an adult that you are pleased or relieved that your parents got divorced—finally—or that you are completely indifferent to the event as long as it doesn't mean you have to change schools or have *your* life cast into turmoil. It is especially difficult when all around you people are tut-tutting and shaking their heads and feeling sorry for you because your parents decided to get unmarried. So, a lot of children play along:

> *"I remember that I liked all the attention. I knew everyone felt sorry for us kids. People were a lot nicer to us because our parents were getting divorced. I don't remember being conscious of the fact that I actually preferred this to the way things were before, but I know that for instance at birthdays and Christmas things definitely improved in the gift department both from my mother*

and my father. I know that my younger sister particularly used to
wheedle extra things and special trips out of my dad by letting
him see how unhappy she was about the divorce. But when he
wasn't around she was just fine."

Of course not every child takes his or her parents' divorce well, but the majority of Solomon's Children handled
their parents' divorce better than most people might have
expected. They saw the situation for what it was and grew
up to be normal mothers and fathers with children of their
own. Few of them lingered excessively over the negative
emotions that most of us feel when we lose something or
somebody dear to us. Most adapted well, and the majority
expressed some concern as to what all the fuss was about in
the first place.

CHILDREN'S TRUE FEELINGS ABOUT DIVORCE

There were several questions in the questionnaire that asked
the respondents how they felt at a certain point in the divorce process (for instance, when they first knew their parents were getting separated or divorced) and how they felt
about the situation in later years. There were also more specific questions, such as "Did you ever feel responsible for your
parents' divorce?" as well as more general questions, such as
how they feel about divorce generally. In addition there were
two separate questions that presented a list of twenty-four
adjectives, each describing a particular feeling. Of these feelings, ten were intended to describe a relatively negative state
of mind, nine a relatively positive state, and the remaining
five were neither particularly negative nor positive and could
be described as just different. Each list of adjectives was presented twice, once at the end of the section on divorce and

the second time at the very end of the questionnaire. It was thought that by repeating the list in this fashion a change in these feelings over time might become evident. Those who filled out the questionnaire were asked to "circle which of the following words best describes your feelings about your parents' divorce AT THE TIME" and then, at the end of the questionnaire, "circle which of the following words best describes your feelings about your parents' divorce NOW." The list of feelings is as follows:

guilty	relieved	normal
abandoned	pleased	interested
happy	indifferent	annoyed
secure	disloyal	blameless
threatened	sad	rejected
satisfied	content	anxious
different	important	embarrassed
puzzled	hurt	fortunate

Some respondents circled several words, others only one or two. In a few cases, where they were too young to have had any particular feeling about the divorce at the time, they circled words only in the last question. Following is a summary of their responses.

Twenty-three percent of the respondents had generally positive feelings about their parents' divorce at the time it occurred as well as in the present. Nineteen percent indicated that their feelings about the divorce were generally negative both at the time it happened and in the present. However, 58 percent had a positive change in reaction between the time of their parents' divorce and the time they filled out the questionnaire—that is, their feelings at the time were generally negative but now they were generally positive. In other words, overall, 81 percent of the respondents said that they now had generally positive feelings about their parents' divorce. This would not seem to indicate a long-lasting negative effect of divorce on the children involved.

The most frequent time lapse between filling out the questionnaire and the parents' divorce was five years. However, the average time lapse was sixteen years; in some cases it was as little as three years, and the longest was forty-seven years. There seemed to be no correlation between the length of time since the divorce occurred and the existence of a generally positive attitude toward it. More time passing, therefore, does not necessarily mean a better adjustment. In fact, quite the opposite. For those who had a really unfortunate experience with their parents' divorce, the feelings and the memories lingered on after many many years.

On the other hand, this young woman is sixteen now. Her parents were divorced only three years ago:

> *"They had always argued, as far back as I can remember. Upon entering junior high I knew that a divorce was inevitable. When two people stop loving each other I don't feel they should stay married. I think they handled it in the most painless way possible."*

The following answer came from a woman of forty-seven who was nine when her parents got divorced. She has been a "child of divorce" for over thirty-eight years, and even though her parents are now both dead she still feels about the divorce the way she did when it happened:

> *"I was nine. I did not really understand what was going on except that it was not 'normal' in my time and age group. I remember a sense of bewilderment and disorientation. I still feel different from other people because of their divorce even though it is now so many years ago."*

An important point to note, however, is not so much the distance in time from the occurrence of the divorce as much as the difference in the generational perspectives about divorce in general. The older respondents who grew up in a time when divorce was something to be ashamed of still have those feelings about it. Whereas those people who were younger seem better able to cope, perhaps because they have grown up in a time when divorce is more acceptable and more common.

Although the respondents were of vastly different ages when they filled out the questionnaire (the youngest being eleven and the oldest sixty-one), the majority of them were within the same age range at the time their parents were divorced—young enough to be dependent on their parents and therefore be part of the divorce itself.

In this study 70 percent of the respondents were between seven and fifteen years old when their parents divorced. Eighty-five percent were between five and twenty years of age. None were older than twenty-five at the time of the divorce.

Because the majority of respondents seemed to fall into two basic age groups at the time of the divorce (those under ten years of age and those between eleven and twenty), it was decided, in examining the frequency of the various feelings circled by the respondents, to look for possible age-related differences between the two groups.

Responses were quite different between the different age groups. For instance, at the time of the divorce, those who were under ten tended to list feelings such as abandoned, puzzled, disloyal, and rejected most often. Those from ten to twenty listed different, puzzled, relieved, and embarrassed with the greatest frequency. Both groups listed sad and hurt with about the same frequency.

Others listed such feelings at the time as: guilty, 23 per-

Most Frequently Felt Emotions About Parents' Divorce for All Ages

---

At the Time		Now	
Feeling	Percentage	Feeling	Percentage
Sad	63%	Blameless	46%
Puzzled	53	Content	44
Hurt	49	Fortunate	41
Different	37	Relieved	40
Abandoned	37	Satisfied	37
Rejected	36	Secure	37
Embarrassed	35	Happy	35
Relieved	34	Sad	32
Disloyal	26	Pleased	28

---

cent; anxious, 14 percent; annoyed, 13 percent; important, 10 percent; threatened, 8 percent; and pleased, 7 percent.

For those who selected the feelings that were neither pro nor con, 19 percent said they felt indifferent at the time of the divorce and 27 percent said they felt indifferent now. Four percent said they felt normal at the time of the divorce and 25 percent said they felt normal now.

FREQUENTLY EXPRESSED FEELINGS

Sad

Sadness was the most frequently listed feeling at the time of the divorce, and some people felt this way even years later. This is understandable because, in effect, the children involved are going through a time of mourning the death of a particular family structure. In addition, children are often mourning the loss of one or both parents. They may feel the loss of their father, usually the absentee parent, acutely, and at the same time may feel that their mother's love and attention are also missing from their lives. How long this mourning process continues seems to be up to both the particular parents involved and the prevailing societal attitude at the time. In those cases where there is a concerted effort to re-create another suitable family structure, even if it is only with one parent, the feelings of sadness and loss are more quickly and easily dealt with.

Those who appeared to feel the sadness most were those who permanently lost contact with a parent or perhaps brothers, sisters, or extended family members because of the divorce and those who grew up at a time when divorce was perceived strongly as being the end not only of a marriage but of the possibility of a normal family life. Fortunately for many children of divorce today this attitude is not as prevalent as it once was. With the remarriage rate climbing, there is no longer a need for the child to expect that family life cannot be resumed even though it may include different participants.

"I think the hardest thing of all was the severing of certain emotional and family ties. It really is sad to think that after thirty years of marriage the whole thing could just be packed in like changing shoes or getting a new car."

"I felt sad because I wanted to have a family like everyone else. I missed the closeness and the feeling that you had two parents who loved each other."

"The saddest part for me was not having my dad when I was a child. I missed him so much and wanted to stay with him. Mom said he didn't want us, and then years later I found out that he had tried to get custody and couldn't. He's gone now, and in a way I still feel cheated that I didn't have all those years with him."

"My sister and I grew apart because I sided with my mother and she with my father. It was sad to lose that close relationship we had before the divorce."

"I missed my grandparents a lot. After my mother remarried I never saw my father's parents again."

"Divorce wasn't something you talked about in those days. Even my mother's family wouldn't talk about what happened, so I grew up feeling different and trying to hide my feelings."

"I haven't seen my father for twenty-seven years. I don't even know where he is or if he is still alive. Sometimes I look at a man on the street who looks like me and I wonder if that's him and why he didn't come after me when mother took us away. I've never been able to figure out whether he loved me or not."

Puzzled

Another often cited feeling was that of puzzlement. Many children said they knew that their parents were having problems with their relationship, but they did not know why. Others complained because no one told them about the divorce until it was all over. They felt left out and confused about what the implications of the divorce would be for them.

"No one told us anything. We came home from school one day and Dad was gone. My mother tried to say he was on a business trip but then a few weeks later she said they were getting a divorce and that was all she ever said about it. I wish they had been more honest with us about what was happening."

"I couldn't understand how parents could not love each other any more."

"My mother sent me to stay with relatives. When I came back two months later it was all over and she wouldn't talk about it. She still won't discuss it even now ten years later."

"No one told me how it was going to affect me. They were all too busy thinking about how it was going to affect their lives. I wanted to know if we would have to move or if I would have to change schools. It was like they ignored me the whole time."

"Everyone I knew had a daddy. I didn't know how we were going to get by without one."

Many parents feel that they are protecting their children by not telling them what is going on, but children often suspect there is a problem and if they are not supplied with correct information they can concoct some pretty fantastic ideas of their own that may do more harm in the long run than knowing the truth. Most children were extremely grateful when their parents leveled with them. It made them feel a part of an important process in their own lives and also allayed a lot of their fears:

"Mom and Dad took the three of us to dinner. Then they explained that they were not going to be married any more and that we children would live with mother. They both told us that their decision had nothing to do with how they felt about us and that even though they were divorced they were still our parents."

Of course there can be too much of a good thing, and telling children more about the divorce than they need to know may also have its detrimental effects:

"My mother told us that Dad left because he had been fooling around with another woman and that he loved her more than he loved us."

"My father told us that Mom had been cheating on him for years and he had finally had enough."

"Mom said that Dad was a fag and that he shouldn't have gotten married in the first place."

"My mother said that Dad was an alcoholic and that's why they had to get divorced. Dad said she was schizophrenic."

Rejected

Another frequently experienced feeling was that of rejection. Many younger children felt that the parent leaving home was also emotionally leaving them. This was particularly true in cases where the dissolution of the marriage was not properly explained to the children. It was even worse in cases where the remaining parent would blame the other parent's departure on the child. One mother told her eleven-year-old that Daddy had left because he didn't love *her* any more. This was obviously a very cruel thing to say and understandably left a lasting impression on the child.

Male children in particular tended to feel some form of rejection not only from their departing fathers but also from their mothers. In some cases mothers would transfer their angry feelings for the father onto the remaining male child. This was also true in the case of daughters who looked like their fathers or who had been accepted generally by the family as being "Daddy's Little Girl."

"I really felt that when my father left my mother he was also leaving me. I was afraid that it was something I had done that caused him to go. It took a long time before I realized that he left the marriage not me and that he still loved me even though he didn't love my mother any more."

"My mother always said I looked just like my father. That was good before the divorce, but after she used to say it whenever she was mad about something he had done, as though she were mad at me too."

"I was always Daddy's girl, and after he left I felt a definite chill on the part of my mother toward me though not toward my brother and sisters. When she would get mad at me she would always say things like 'Why don't you go and live with your father, you're just like him.' "

Embarrassed

Feelings of embarrassment seemed to be most prevalent for those who were in their early to middle teenage years at the time of the divorce. This is understandable on many levels. First, teenagers are having trouble coping with their own day to day crises of growing up. They are at an age when peer opinion is very important. They want very much to be like everybody else. Having parents who are doing something that is unusual or hard to explain to one's friends can be a great source of personal embarassment. If the divorce is not being handled well by the parents and there are messy scenes, especially in public, embarrassment is also natural.

Embarrassment is more likely to be felt by the child who is the only one of his circle to have divorcing parents. It makes him feel different and may direct undesired attention his way both from peers as well as teachers, relatives, and others. In the aftermath of the divorce, too, many teens wish their parents would handle dating and remarriage with more aplomb. It can be embarrassing when you are discovering your own sexuality to find out that your newly divorced parents are also *re*discovering theirs. Seeing your parents as sexual beings can be rough for teenagers of divorce. And too, should newly remarried parents suddenly report the impending arrival of a half-sibling who is twelve or fifteen years your junior, embarrassment is a definite possibility.

Most teenagers like to put their parents on the back burner of life. It is part of their growing process, part of their way of asserting their own independence as budding adults. To find that your parents are coming to the forefront of things, hogging the limelight as it were by getting divorced and remarried just when you see yourself as the center of attention, is understandably difficult.

"I remember being very embarrassed when my teachers at school used to treat me differently because my parents were divorced. I just wanted to be treated like all the other kids."

"It was very embarrassing for me when my date would come to pick me up and my mother's 'date' would arrive at the same time. There were a lot of awkward silences, believe me."

"I was embarrassed that my parents, at their ages, were getting divorced in the first place. I think I felt they were selfish to do that and that they had no business thinking about themselves, just me."

"My parents always had loud, loud fights and I remember shouting at them to shut up and stop fighting. I was so afraid the neighbors would hear. And after one of their fights I was too embarrassed to walk down the street."

"I think the most embarrassing thing was that my father married a woman twelve years younger than himself and at the age of forty-eight he became a father again when he should have been thinking about being a grandfather."

A CASE OF PARENTAL SEDUCTION?

Disloyal

Many children of divorce, no matter what their age at the time, report feelings of divided loyalties or of disloyalty to one parent. In this study 74 percent of the people said they felt they were forced to choose between one parent and the other at the time of the divorce. Many were able to withstand the pressure to choose, but several still felt they were put in a position where they were forced to be disloyal to one of their parents. Parental seduction—the encouragement of one or sometimes both parents to "take my side" in the divorce—is all too common. It can be very injurious to the children involved because they are forced to treat love as a commodity that can be apportioned and divided according to someone else's picture of reality. Being forced to choose the parent you love more is as cruel as asking the parents to choose the child they love the most and then discard the others.

"My father would always give me money whenever I went to visit him. It was like we both understood that this money was 'paying' for my visiting him. I guess he thought he had to buy me or I wouldn't have come to see him."

"My mother was always telling me how bad my father was. I knew she felt that if I thought he was bad enough I wouldn't love him any more, just her."

"I think my mother always tried to justify her leaving my father by telling me he was lazy and no good, etc. Maybe she thought if I believed it then it would be true. The real fact of the matter was that she regretted leaving him and had to find a way to justify it to herself. I knew she was trying to make me stop loving him."

"My mother said that I couldn't love my stepmother and her. So after a while I didn't talk about my stepmother any more because I knew that if my mother knew how much I really loved her she would be very upset."

"I told my parents straight out that there was no use them trying to get me to take sides. I loved them both because they were my parents and I just refused to get involved in their little games."

"After the divorce their behavior toward me changed. It was like they were vying to see which one could give me more presents or more outings so that I would favor one more than the other. It was disgusting."

GUILTY AS CHARGED?

Many people believe that children feel guilty about their parents' divorce—that in some way they blame themselves for the ending of the marriage. I did not find this to be the case. On the contrary, the most frequently selected feeling that the respondents now had about the divorce was blame-lessness. I think that most of them realized that their parents' marital troubles had little or nothing to do with them, even though some parents tried to convince their children of the contrary.

ONE MORE TIME?

Some of those who feel that children experience a consider-able sense of guilt over the dissolution of their parents' marriage point to the fact that children invariably seek to reunite their parents and that, in many cases, they try to bring about reconciliation in order to alleviate their own sense of guilt about the break-up.

Indeed, it would seem that if divorce is a life-wrenching event for children, then the majority of them would probably prefer to see their parents reunited and the old family life routine re-established.

It was surprising, then, to find out that when asked if they hoped their parents would be reconciled and if they had ever done anything to encourage a reconciliation, 67.5 percent of the respondents gave a very emphatic "No."

"I hoped that the two sides of the family would stop fighting but I never hoped for a reconciliation betwen my parents. There was no need for them to get back together, so why bother?"

"No. I just wished that the fighting would stop and that someone would talk to me."

"No. I hoped that my mother would drop dead so that I could go and live with my father."

"No. It would have been foolish. I wanted them to get divorced because I recognized that these two people no longer had anything in common."

"Both my brother and I hoped that all the arguing and bad feeling would end. It was not for us to help them reconcile. We were not the ones living in their marriage. We were just products of an unfortunate incident."

"I really had no thoughts about it. I remember reading about kids who had tried to get their parents back together. I thought they were dumb."

"No, of course not. If there was a chance they would get back to-gether a) they would have done it by themselves, b) it was not my place, c) I never really thought of it."

"I never hoped they would even try to get back together. If they did I was just afraid that it would start all over again."

"Why would I want them to get back together. They were so much happier apart?"

Most of the respondents, even though some were quite young at the time, seemed to have had a more matter-of-fact attitude toward the whole process of their parents' divorce than is popularly believed. Many of them reflected that rec-onciliation was not part of their job as children, and others were just glad to have some peace and quiet for a change or to see their parents happy at last. They did not seek reconcil-iation but accepted the breakdown of the marriage as an ir-refutable fact. This adaptive attitude on the part of the children may make us question some of our beliefs about the ultimate importance of our marriage to our children.

FEELINGS IN THE LONG TERM

It is evident that for most people there was a change in how they felt about their parents' divorce over time. In the major-ity of cases, negative feelings such as rejection and aban-donment were replaced over time with feelings such as contentment, satisfaction, security, and relief.

Relief

Relief was reported by some people at the time of the di-vorce, but even more respondents expressed that feeling when they examined how they felt about the divorce in the present. The fact that children of divorce can feel relief is perhaps not as highly publicized as their feelings of sadness or rejection, for instance, because to do so would be to admit that divorce can be a good thing. However, the fact that even very young children can experience a ceasing of tension with the divorce of their parents shows that such old opinions as "we can pretend everything is all right and the children won't be any the wiser" and "even a bad marriage is better than coming from a broken home" do not hold water.

Some studies have shown that even children as young as six months can detect marital disharmony and react to the stress. As they grow older more and more children become aware of what is going on in their home, and it can be frightening for them if their parents pretend everything is all right when in fact the air is thick with tension:

"My parents started having marital problems when I was four or five. Instead of fighting they had these cold, cold silences. When I was about six they started to sleep in separate bedrooms. They lived that way until I left home at twenty-one, all the while pretending that everything was O.K. between them. The worst part of it is not only that they wasted all those years pretending when they would have been happier apart but that my brothers and I grew up thinking that all marriages were cold and distant like theirs. Both of my brothers are divorced and I can't see ever getting married myself."

"Everybody relaxed when they finally got divorced. They are both much nicer people now that they don't spend all their time arguing with each other."

Fortunate

Some may say that relief is merely an emotional state in which, because of time, there is now an absence of the need for negative feelings and that there are no truly positive effects of divorce. That is not so, according to several of the respondents.

Most people do not associate feeling fortunate with coming from a "broken home." But when you ask people who have actually been through the divorce of their parents, you find that many of them do report feeling fortunate:

"I know that I would not have been the independent and understanding person I am today if I had not been the child of a divorced home. It forced me to grow up sooner and also to understand more about relationships."

"If my parents had not gotten divorced, I would not have been so careful in my own choice of a mate. As it is, I looked long and hard and knew what to look for as a result of seeing how they had chosen people who were completely wrong for them."

"Being a child of divorce and divorced myself, I think I was much more prepared to handle the situation with my children because I knew what they were feeling. As a result of that I think that they have grown up to be well-adjusted and loving human beings with no divorce scars."

"My second wife is a child of divorce and as such she knows what it is like to be a stepchild so she is really terrific with her own stepchildren. I think our marriage would have been more difficult if she had come from a so-called 'normal' home."

"I feel fortunate because I got to know both of my parents as people because they got divorced. If they had stayed together I

don't think I would have liked either of them as much as I do now."

"*The divorce brought me closer not only to my brothers and sisters but to my other family as well. We all kind of pulled together, and even now, years later, that feeling of closeness is still there. I don't think it would have been that way if my parents had stayed together.*"

"*I was the first kid on the block so to speak whose parents got divorced, but two years later when some of my friend's parents started to get divorced I was able to help them out because I had been through it all.*"

As we have said before, children are not stupid but they are resilient, and with warm and loving parents, the so-called negative effects of divorce can be minimal while the positive ones can last a lifetime.

HOW THE FEELINGS OF ADULTS FIT IN

The problem with most adults when they think about divorce and its effects on children is that they are usually thinking about it while they are going through it. They are in a state of great emotional upheaval themselves and often project their own anxieties onto their children. It seems to keep them company in some odd way. Also, their own perceptions of divorce were learned in another era, when the dissolution of a marriage was looked on as something incredibly suspect, something to be ashamed of at the very least. They may be inclined to forget, therefore, that the children of the eighties who are feeling the full force of the rising divorce rate are not in any sense as naïve about the situation as their parents were or are. Children these days see divorce all around them. It is not a foreign concept nor is it something that tends to set them apart from their peers. Many of them see divorce as just another possible facet of family life.

When it comes to emotions and divorce it is the parents who are having the problems, not the children. They are the ones who cannot handle the situation. If children fall victim to the feelings of divorce at all, they are victims of their parents' feelings, not their own, like the little girl in the following story, reported in Los Angeles by Liz Hodgson in 1984. It is a sad testament to what can happen to a child in the divorce process just because her parents cannot deal with their own feelings:

> *The parents of Samantha, a five-year-old only child, argued over who would have custody of the child when their stormy marriage broke up. The mother swore that she would not give the child up. The father was heartbroken.*
>
> *When they met to discuss the arrangement there was more arguing, and the mother took the child back to her car to drive her home. The father took the girl from the car and went to his own vehicle. The enraged mother tried to run him down, but he was able to make it to his van with the child.*
>
> *Then began a chase fueled by hatred and revenge. The mother rammed her car into the back of the father's van and tried to push it off the road even though the terrified child was in the front seat of the van. The father drew a gun and fired at the mother's car. Shortly afterward, both vehicles went out of control and the van rolled over and over into a ditch. The little girl was thrown from the van.*
>
> *Five days later she died of her injuries. Both parents survived.*
>
> *The attorney, Vladimir Kozina, who is prosecuting the case for the state, was quoted as saying, "This case is disgusting. The little girl was just a helpless pawn in her parents' battles with each other. Now she is dead."*

DIVORCE—A RITE OF PASSAGE?

The majority of children of divorce are rarely as severely affected as they are made out to be. Youngsters or teenagers or young adults, they proved, for the most part, that they were not only resilient when it came to being the children of "broken homes" but very practical as well. There was not a great deal of longing to put things back the way they had been or a great deal of feeling "if only things could have been different." There was, however, a lot of acceptance of the way things were. These people perceived their parents' divorce not so much as a brick wall that barred their way to a normal growing process but as one of many possible stepping stones on the path to adulthood.

If we are to concern ourselves with the long-term effects of divorce on children, then let us look to the way adults mishandle the divorce situation, for it is the emotions they invoke for it rather than the existence of the divorce itself that has the most lasting effect on the children involved.

Chapter Eight

The Future Family

I believe that more unhappiness comes from this source [the family] than from any other—I mean from the attempt to prolong family connections unduly and to make people hang together artificially who would never naturally do so.

Samuel Butler

I have seen the future and it works.

Lincoln Steffens

The days when a man and a woman and the children of their union comprised the structure of the "normal" family are over. Today, one in six American families is a stepfamily. One in five children under the age of eighteen lives in a stepfamily situation. By 1990 single-parent and stepparent families combined will outnumber those with two natural parents.

Because of a predicted rise in the divorce rate to more than 50 percent of marriages in the next five years, these figures can only be expected to increase. When you consider that 60 percent of divorced persons have children under eighteen and that five out of six divorced men and three out of four divorced women remarry, 50 percent within the first three years after the divorce, then it is time we reassess our concept of what constitutes "normal" family life.

In a paper presented at the Ackerman Institute for Family Therapy in New York in 1984, social worker Anita Morawetz suggested that in view of the rising divorce rate, divorce and separation should be viewed as normal phases of family life, not aberrations:

> Are we ready to think of separation and divorce as one of many possible stages of the family life cycle that people are likely to experience, another developmental phase that has to be successfully mastered in order to pass on to the next one? Can we become more comfortable with the issues of loss, separation, breakdown of marriage? Maybe we have to begin finding new words for old phenomena. Perhaps instead of calling it marital breakdown, with its connotation of failure and danger, we could think in terms of a couple's being "ready for a new relationship" or of the contract on which the marriage was based as "having been completed." Instead of perceiving children as the unwilling, helpless victims of a trauma, it may be more useful to view them as facing the challenge of handling a number of significant adult relationships or being the lucky possessors of two families instead of one.

Morawetz suggested that rather than trying to change what is, we should adapt our thinking to accommodate the reality of the new family structure where divorce and remarriage play an integral part.

A large part of our problem in coping with the new shape of the family is that many nay sayers would still prefer to believe that divorce is an antifamily institution that is going to cause the corruption and eventual disintegration of our society. In fact, the majority of those who get divorced try marriage again and even again if necessary. The current rate of remarriage is an endorsement of our belief in the union itself and the value of family life. We must stop looking at divorce as "The End" and subsequent marriages as being less valid or important. For, at the root of it all, our motives in getting divorced and remarried are not destructive but constructive. Sometimes it is necessary to tear something down in order to build something better.

It is because of our desire to create a harmonious family life that is satisfying for *all* concerned that we reformat our personal relationships as couples. Because marriage is the basis of the family structure, we must change the shape and often the content of what we have been calling "the traditional family structure" but should be calling "the old family structure." Indeed, there are so many combinations of viable family relationships today that it is no longer possible to say, "That one works and is acceptable" and "That one is not." We can no longer justifiably measure the worth of a family relationship by its symmetry. Conformity in family life is not a hallmark of success. The only rule by which we should be measuring the adequacy of any family is whether or not it works for those involved.

Unfortunately, most of the people who make our laws and policies still regard the traditional nuclear family structure as the only right and viable format for the family. They spend time and effort trying to force their own and other people's "future families" back into a format where, like a shoe two sizes too small, the situation not only will be uncomfortable but may be downright unhealthy.

We need only to look at our negative and unrealistic perceptions of the stepfamily to see how resistant most people are to the existence of the "future family." But the stepfamily is a harbinger of what we can expect of family life in the future. By the end of this century stepfamilies will outnumber "traditional families." It is time therefore to take a closer look at this situation, which is more often than not the result of divorce and which affects the lives of the "children of divorce" profoundly.

THE SERIAL MARRIAGE

Those who marry, divorce, and remarry are often regarded as somewhat suspect, as if their inability to "get it right the first time" means they may never be able to get it right at all. We do not have a lot of faith in the value of second marriages. We do not give those involved in them much encouragement. If any of these people should try a third marriage, we would think them truly inadequate personalities, selfish, immature, spoiled, and unable to face the give and take of married life.

It is a curious thing, the way we perceive people's attempts to enjoy a second or third married relationship. Instead of considering them to be failures, why can we not instead congratulate them on having so many loving relationships in one lifetime? We cannot yet accept that marriages can break down or wear out and that it is not necessarily the fault of those who participated in them.

The absolutist concept of one man, one woman for life is outdated. Just as the idea of having one job or living in one town for an entire life is foreign to many Americans of the eighties, so should be the idea of having only one acceptable spouse in a lifetime. We allow people to change freely from job to job, house to house, even country to country in many cases, with no recriminations. But should they try that with marriage, well, there must be something wrong with them. As a culture we embrace change in every area but that of marriage and family life. We still expect people to marry for life. If they can no longer maintain that relationship, we punish them financially, emotionally, and socially, and we hold the children they have now and the children they may have in the future accountable too.

It is no surprise then that those children who are the product of their parents' second marriage are frequently regarded as interlopers in the family not only by other family members but by the law as well. Many parents who have children from a second marriage have written me to ask why these children were not welcomed by other members of the family. One woman said that her mother made a terrible fuss over the two children from her first marriage because she regarded them as her "real grandchildren," but the two children from her second marriage and her stepchildren were completely ignored. Other families have told me that various lawyers and judges have told them that the children of the first marriage come first and that any subsequent children have to take a back seat whether it be financially or personally. An example of this type of mentality is given by Judge Charles McClure of Tallahassee: "They [the children of the first marriage] come before any subsequent children, before any second marriage."

How can we place a value on children just because of their order in the birth and marriage hierarchy? This harks back to the days when first sons got everything and second sons nothing or sons inherited and daughters did not. Though we would consider that extremely unfair these days, and in fact the law provides that all children shall inherit equally, we still discriminate against children of subsequent marriages. The stigma of being illegitimate has been almost completely removed, but the stigma of being the child of a second or third marriage remains strong. Should we continue to blame these children for existing?

We cannot go hiding our heads in the sand forever. There will continue to be subsequent marriages and children from these unions. Many sociologists predict that we can reasonably expect three marriages in an average lifetime by the end of this century. Today's stepfamily situation is a forerunner of the "future family," where it will be "normal" to have a mixture of children by different marriages.

In 1920 men had a life expectancy of fifty-three years,

women of fifty-four. In 1980, these ages had increased to seventy and seventy-eight, respectively. The days when being married for a lifetime meant twenty or twenty-five years are long gone. It was much easier for a marriage to last a lifetime when a lifetime was not much longer than the time it took to raise children to adulthood. Nowadays people tend to marry in their early twenties. By the time they reach their mid-forties their children are gone, and they then face another thirty years alone again as a couple. Because of our increasing longevity we would be better off if we could accept the fact that many of us will marry more than once, that these marriages may have children, and that they are just as valid and important and real as the marriage or marriages that preceded them. It is time we stopped judging the validity of the marriage by its priority and started judging it by its quality.

TAKING STEPS

A couple in Florida had been married happily for fifteen years. One day their daughter came home from school and demanded to know why she didn't have stepparents like all the other kids. It seems that those who had extra sets of parents got more attention, more presents, and generally had more opportunity for fun than the kids who just had two parents.

It is encouraging that children have the resilience to accept, adjust to, and even see the benefits of new situations while adults talk about wicked stepmothers and their unfortunate charges. In our study, 69 percent of the respondents reported that they liked their stepmothers and 44 percent said they liked their stepfathers. Taking steps into your life does not have to result in the emotional starvation that is so often pictured as typical of a stepfamily situation.

"I only have one stepparent and she is my favorite. I really love her a lot and her new baby."

"I really love my stepfather. And my stepmother and I have an amicable relationship though I must say I was a little resentful when she had two new kids. I thought it was disruptive to the family."

"I never met Dad's second wife but wife number three is great— a lovely lady and a good friend. My stepfather and I buried the hatchet years ago and now we truly care for each other."

"I hated her at first but later on we began to work things out and now we get along just fine."

"They both remarried soon after the divorce. My dad's new wife is really nice. She is really dear, just like a friend. I liked her immediately. I had a lot of respect for my mom's husband. He cared for us a great deal but I didn't really love him."

"My stepmother is a wonderful person. I wish she had been my mother. She is a great grandmother to my children, a loving, caring person, intelligent and business minded."

"At first I didn't care for her. Then I blamed her for breaking up their marriage even though I really knew she didn't. Now, she has become a very important person in my life and I love her deeply."

"My stepfather is a very kind, polite man. I like him a lot but I don't feel close to him the way I did with my dad."

Most of these "children of divorce" accepted their step-parents, and even if they did not love them as they did their parents they liked them as people. In some cases one stepparent was preferred to another. If that was the case, stepmothers had a slight edge. Forty percent of the respondents said they preferred their stepmother while only 36 percent said they preferred their stepfather. Twenty-four percent said they had no preference. There were also those who made no bones about the fact that they did not care for their stepparents at all. Fortunately, they were in the minority.

"I hated my stepfather but I came to love and care for my step-mother."

"As a rule, I disliked them. My first stepmother insulted my mother constantly. My second stepmother and I are just incompatible as personalities. My stepfather was an O.K. person but he made a lazy and unfair parent."

"I thought he was a wimp but he usually treated us O.K. He was lazy though. Dad was only married a few months before he died, but his wife was a two-faced bitch and she talked too much."

"As a stepmother now myself I can see how difficult it must have been for my stepmother dealing with my brothers and me. Quite frankly there are times when I could cheerfully strangle my husband's children, but then there are times I have felt that way about my own children too."

OTHER PEOPLE'S CHILDREN

Just as not all stepparents can be viewed as compatible people, so the same is true of step-siblings. Fifty-two percent of the respondents had positive feelings about their step-siblings and 15 percent said they were indifferent or did not know them well enough to feel one way or the other. Some of the respondents preferred some step-siblings to others. Few disliked all their step-siblings categorically. As with stepparents, it seemed to be a question of successfully matching personalities. Those who found their step-siblings to be like themselves or to have qualities they admired had few problems adjusting, but those who found a wide personality gap naturally found it difficult to accept the others as being part of the family. This is a verity, of course, not only among step-siblings but among children who were born to the same mother and father. It is unfortunately a fact of life and does not necessarily reflect in an adverse way on the stepfamily situation.

> *"My father had four children from his second wife, none from wife number three. My mother has four from her second hubby. I'm very fond of Mom's children and very close to them. My father's kids, on the other hand, are 'blood-sucking twerps.' "*

> *"My stepmother's daughter was retarded, so I thought she was weird but O.K. I tried to keep my distance. Then they had one of their own. Since I had been the baby of the family, I felt the new baby was an intruder. I was thirteen when he was born and he was a bit of a novelty, but I resented the extra work I had to do because of him. I thought Mom was rather old to be having another kid too. After all she was thirty-six."*

> *"My three stepsisters are real JAPS (Jewish American princesses). They hardly have any personality or sense of humor between the three of them. They're not a bit like my mom and me."*

> *"The younger one is O.K. At least she's level-headed, but the older one is a spoiled rotten brat—totally self-centered."*

"It was very hard to get used to having a younger brother and sister though they accepted me very easily, and now I love them as my real family."

"After a couple of years Mom had my halfbrother and I was a little jealous at first. But he was only a baby and babies are so easy to love, so I didn't blame him. I have only met one of my stepfather's children because they are older than me so I don't really know if I like them or not."

"I think my stepbrother and stepsister are spoiled and very vain, but we all try to get along even though we are so different."

"I've never met two people like my stepbrothers in my whole life. They are so completely different from me, different attitudes, different beliefs. I really have nothing in common with them, and I wouldn't have anything to do with them if they were not stepfamily."

OTHER PEOPLE'S PEOPLE

In most stepfamily situations it is not just the parents and custodial or visiting children who are the main players. There are also ex-spouses to be dealt with and ex-in-laws. This is the area of greatest difficulty for most people involved in a stepfamily situation, adults and children alike. The relationships between the parents and their ex-spouses and their new partners is crucial to making a happy stepfamily situation. If the relationship is marked by a reasonably civilized approach on the part of the adults, the children will relax and benefit from the presence of several loving, caring "parents" in their lives. But if the terms of the relationship are bad, the children become confused, feel pushed into taking sides, and generally experience the tension of not knowing who is right. In cases like this, instead of having two natural parents who are constantly fighting and creating a stressful environment, they now have four—double jeopardy.

In this study, the respondents reported that the relationship between their custodial parent and their separated parent's new spouse was more apt to be bad than good. Only 14 percent said that their significant adults were on good terms. Forty-five percent said that the feelings ran high and negative between the adults involved, and a further 41 percent said there was no relationship at all between their stepparent and their custodial parent.

"My mother called my stepmother names—'whore,' etc.—to her face. She was not often entirely negative about her, but usually behind her back. It seemed entertaining at the time, but now I am not so sure."

"Things are very, very touchy between all of them. I blame my mom for keeping up with this open marriage business, but I try not to get involved. Really, it is their problem."

"Mom hated my stepmother though I don't think they ever really met. So I hated her too, but not any more. I still don't like her though."

"They all tried to be as reasonable as possible about everything. It made life much easier for me because I didn't have to take sides."

"They fight like cats and dogs. Mom once saw my stepmother driving 'Dad's' car, and when she parked it my mom got in and drove it away! Her attitude made life very tough for me because I liked my stepmother a lot."

"When my first child was born my mother and my stepmother both came to the hospital at the same time and went to the nursery to see the baby. My stepmother put her hand on my mother's arm to congratulate her. My mother reacted as if she had been touched by a leper and left the hospital building immediately. I felt sorry for my mother that she could be so hateful at such a joyous time. She missed so much she could have had."

"My father and stepfather are like black and white. They make sure they are never in a situation that requires relating. To me it seems childish, but that is really their problem."

"They wouldn't attend the same family functions. Everyone had to phone around beforehand to make sure that so and so wasn't coming. If one showed up, the other left. My cousin's wedding was a fiasco. It made me very nervous about any sort of 'family' occasion. So when I got married I didn't invite any of them, stepparents or parents, just some friends and my sister. I didn't want their stupidity to spoil my wedding."

"My grandparents refuse to speak to or of my stepmother. They still refer to my mother as my father's wife and refuse to acknowledge the baby he had with my stepmother. It makes me feel I have to watch what I say and that I can't express my real feelings because I know it would upset them if I said nice things about my stepmother or my halfbrother."

"They were great friends. My mother said she always liked Elaine and didn't blame her for anything. It made me respect my mother an awful lot for having such a mature attitude."

Only 14 percent of the respondents in this survey said they felt good about the relationship between their natural parents and their stepparents. All those whose stepparents and natural parents were on bad terms said that it made them feel very uncomfortable. Some, who initially aped one of their parents' negative opinion of the other's new spouse, changed their minds over time even though the relationship between the adults remained static. Most children had a mind of their own when it came to their feelings about step-relatives, and many thought the adults in their lives were being incredibly childish or needlessly negative. Bad feeling between stepparents and natural parents often caused a rift to develop between the respondents and their natural parents because they saw them as being more to blame for the continuing negative state of affairs and judged them accordingly.

Thirty-six percent removed themselves, at least emotionally, from the situation by saying that they were indifferent to the relationship between their stepparents and natural parents. Many of these respondents felt that either it was not their problem or that there was nothing they could do to change things. As the last quote above indicates, in cases where the natural parent acted in an "adult" and reasonable fashion toward the stepparent, the children were inclined to feel more positive not only about their stepparent but about their natural parent too. It would seem then that in order to increase the possibilities of a happy family life for the "children of divorce," adults would be wise not to let their own emotions interfere with their children forming sound relationships with their stepparents or stepgrandparents. There is no rule that says that the maximum number of parents a child can love is two.

In 1985 a letter appeared in Judith Martin's "Miss Manners" column that is a perfect example of how narrow-minded some people can be when it comes to sharing their children with new members of the family. The letter was written by a woman who resented that her stepmother (only referred to by the writer as "my father's new wife") was calling herself the "Grandma" of her father's grandchildren.

The writer pointed out that the children already had two grandmothers who were living and that she thought this was enough. It was clear that because she didn't like her stepmother she didn't want her children to benefit from any sort of close relationship with this woman either. A selfish position indeed.

Fortunately Miss Manners, who has both feet firmly planted in the eighties, answered that a modern child could easily accumulate many grandparents and asked the writer what was wrong with someone new loving her children. This is a good answer that reflects both the current reality and natural common sense.

STEPS AS PARENTS

Some of the respondents thought their stepparents made better parents than their natural parents. One girl said she thought of her natural father as her *bio*logical parent and her stepfather as her logical parent. Others thought the opposite. But how one perceives the parenting skills of an individual is not always related to how one perceives these people as individuals. Many of the respondents in this survey said that the stepparent-as-friend was the ideal role for their natural parent's new spouse to play. Particularly with those who encountered stepparents for the first time as teenagers, uncalled-for interference (too much parenting), lackadaisical parenting (too little or too late), or rules and regulations diametrically opposed to those they had known before were the focus of most of the tension. With younger children, the "you're not my mother (father) so I don't have to listen to you" situation usually occurred when the relationship between natural parents or between natural parents and stepparents was tense. These children were most confused about who was "boss." The parents were the main culprits here because they often sent out confusing messages. For instance, the mother would tell the child that "Daddy was going to come back home someday" and that his new wife would not be around too long. (When asked if one of their parents had tried to get the marriage back together after the divorce, those who said "yes" overwhelmingly cited the mother.) Though this was often wishful thinking on the parent's part, the child perceived it as permission to ignore the "temporary" presence of the interloper and did just that. In cases where it was the stepfather who was ignored, it was because the mother often failed to establish his position in the household for the benefit of the children. She did not take him from the role of "Mommy's boyfriend" to "Mommy's husband" in the children's eyes, so the children tended to treat him as someone who was only passing through. Younger children are particularly susceptible to picking up attitudes from their custodial parent, and where these attitudes concern the new stepparent and are negative, trouble is definitely brewing.

"My stepmother was so bossy. She was always telling us what to do, and we didn't like it one bit."

"I didn't like my stepfather interfering. As far as I was concerned, what I did was my business, not his."

"My mother used to tell us not to pay any attention to my step-mother because she didn't know what she was talking about."

"There were two households with two different sets of rules. My mother was very precise and ran everything like she was the captain of the ship. In my father's house things were much more easygoing. It took some getting used to, living two different ways depending on where you were."

Another facet of stepparenting that can affect how children feel about a new family is the possibility of an obvious preference by the stepparents for their own children from a previous marriage to their stepchildren. Eighty-one percent of the respondents said that not all the children in the new family were treated equally. However, the lines of preference were not always drawn up according to who was blood and who wasn't. In cases where they were, most of the children took a mature view and said that that was perfectly natural.

"My stepfather basically ignored me and my brother, but my mother spoiled his two boys because she was trying to win them over. She never disciplined them so they got away with murder while my brother and I always had to do the work. My mother wanted everyone to get along, and she knew that she could count on my brother and me to pull our weight and she didn't want to upset his boys."

"I found that my father would find fault with all the kids, but my stepmother would get angry at me to get back at him. They both leaned toward their own kids more though. My stepmother now pays attention only to her kids and my father still leans toward me."

"Each parent seemed to prefer and tolerate their own children better. But then this is natural because they were their own."

"I was the favorite of both my parents and my stepparents. It was my brother who got the short end of the stick from both sides."

"My father treated all the children the same. My mother treated us all differently. By the time I had a stepmother it was irrelevant."

"Different children have different wants and needs. I was first, so the rules were always stricter for me. Money was tighter too. But the others were younger and they fought to get their own way more. Time and experience mellow parents too."

"My mother definitely favors me. My step-dad favors his children. That is to be expected."

"I was treated differently. I was always singled out as the problem child because I was the youngest and ostensibly the wildest. My present stepmother tried to form a friendship with my brother and sister but not with me. Generally I was left for the other kids to raise."

"Everyone was tougher on my brother and sister than on me. They were troublemakers, much mouthier, and they were very vocal in their dislike of my stepfather. They gave Mom a real rough time."

"Everyone was treated according to his or her own needs. We are all very different people after all. My youngest brother has a low I.Q. and gets in trouble a lot. My older brother was very bright and gifted—the family son. I was already grown up with a child of my own. I think it was a very common-sense approach to the situation."

"I think it's very hard for a stepparent not to treat their own flesh and blood differently. I know I do with my children and my mother did with me. It's natural."

"My stepmother was never strict with my brother or me. She never interfered or told us what to do. She was never parental with us, but she was to her own children. I think it was because she wanted us to like her."

Sometimes stepparents are harder on their own children, and sometimes on their stepchildren. In some cases one or two children are singled out for different treatment because of their personalities or their ages. Just as with natural families, stepfamilies have their favorites and their black sheep. It is odd, however, that many people are surprised when a stepparent admits to this. We still have the idea that all children should be treated the same in stepfamilies even though that is not the way we generally act in traditional families. Perhaps we should stop categorizing children according to whether they were born into the family or whether they came into it through marriage and start accepting the fact that parents can react to them as people, and we should expect the children to react to their stepparents in the same way. Then the relationships in the "future family" will be a lot more natural for everyone.

STEPFAMILY PLUSES AND MINUSES

Like most situations in life, having a stepfamily has its good side as well as its bad. The important point to make here is that the respondents were aware of and had firsthand experience with the good side, a side not often expounded upon by those who see divorce and its aftermath as an essentially negative experience for children.

As the following table indicates, the positive side of the stepfamily situation was often an improved family life, including such things as having more people to love, exposure to different family systems, a better role model of married life, and more parents.

The respondents were also aware that others were benefitting from the new family and included such things as the parents having someone to love and be with, and a greater opportunity for sharing and communication with other people. On the more self-centered side, they listed positive aspects such as more opportunity to travel (this because the families were often geographically separated), better business contacts, and an improved financial situation.

Of course it is true that some respondents found life a little more difficult with two families to cope with instead of one, but much of this difficulty is related to the problems we all have adapting to change within the routine or structure of even the natural family unit. And, too, not all parents handle the step situation with equal elan and this is bound to affect how the children perceive the situation of having a stepfamily.

Under disadvantages of having a stepfamily the respondents listed difficult family life most often, including different approaches to parenting, unfamiliar family traditions, interference from nonblood members of the family in major issues, parental arguing, and unclear or ambiguous relationships within the new family group.

The second hardest thing for them to deal with was the flow of negative emotions that often accompanied the stepfamily situation. These included jealousy, hostility, anger, distrust, conflict, and resentment. In addition, there were certain situational disadvantages, such as fitting their new family into their old life-style and trying to find time to cope with additional relationships, as well as dealing with social occasions.

On a more personal level, the respondents sometimes reported feeling different from other families (although this is certainly becoming less and less the case today), and feeling inadequate or competitive within the new family structure.

Some of the respondents' comments about the pluses and minuses of having a stepfamily appear on page 161.

Major Advantages		Major Disadvantages	
Improved family life	62%	Difficult family life	41%
Other-centered benefits	21	Negative emotions	32
Self-centered benefits	17	Situational disadvantages	21
		Personal disadvantages	6

"If everyone gets along and there are no hard feelings, it can be pretty nice."

"There are more role models, different perspectives, and more people to talk to, but dividing time can be a big problem!*"*

"There are no problems that I can think of. I get to travel a lot and that's great."

"It certainly is better than no family at all, but sometimes the clash of values and traditions makes life more difficult."

"Sometimes there are too many rules, too much arguing between all the parents, but you get to have another sort of family life and you have the chance of getting a better parent."

"The best thing is that my father is happy and I got exposed to a new type of family life."

"When it's better than the old family it helps to set a better example of marriage. That's what my father's second marriage did for me. But in my own marriage my husband (second) and my two older children do not get along very well, so that is a disadvantage of course."

"I grew up with four parental figures whom I could use for advice, help, etc. But since none of my friends had stepparents, it made me feel different."

"My stepfather is a real peach. He is almost like a surrogate father for me. Besides, it broadens my business contacts. The worst thing is having to juggle holidays between the two families without getting anyone offended."

"It gave me an extended support group. At least there was a man in the house again, which helped aid the finances. But, there is an invisible dividing line between us—a lack of blood—and I don't feel the same responsibilities to accept my stepfather unconditionally as I do my father. It creates a family ambiguity: two fathers? two mothers? and separate philosophies of how to raise children."

"I don't have to feel sorry for my parents because they are lonely. But the clash of family traditions can make it all rather a pain sometimes."

"It's hard to split the time up, especially near the holidays, but then I do have a new stepbrother whom I love dearly."

"I have a sister I didn't have before, but really there are just too many birthdays to keep track of now."

"It is difficult to divide your time, but you do have the chance of finding a family that you like. A lot of kids whose parents don't get divorced are just stuck with what they've got."

YOU DON'T *HAVE* TO LOVE EACH OTHER

Most people have a pie-in-the-sky idea about how stepfamilies are supposed to work. It usually ends up looking something like "The Brady Bunch," where they all love one another equally and they all get along all the time and help and care for each other "just the way real families do."

First of all, that TV image of a family has no more substance than shoot 'em up westerns or game show give-aways. Second, even members of "natural" families—who are all related according to the great nuclear paradigm—don't always feel that way about each other. It's wonderful if it turns out that everyone in the family loves everyone else, but as you can see, some stepchildren love some stepparents better than others and some don't love them at all. Just because a man and a woman decide that they like each other enough to want to get married and share a home does not mean that other members of their families have to like each other as well. If you want to compare stepfamily life to a situation comedy it might be better to look in the direction of "Gilligan's Island," where everyone is different and has different wants and needs that have to be accommodated within a communal structure.

There are two important things to be aware of in a stepfamily situation. One is that you don't all *have* to love each other; and the other is that you can't always make it perfect, no matter how hard you try. Sometimes personality differences are a barrier that cannot be brought down. Sometimes there are bad feelings that have nothing to do with the step-relatives but everything to do with what occurred before they came on the scene. Many adults make the mistake of overcompensating within a stepfamily, as if they have to make up for something or apologize. Many are disappointed because they had expected instant love and affection. Most children who have gone through a stepfamily situation agree that a new family cannot be formed instantly but that time can mold new and often beneficial relationships.

One of the greatest benefits in any stepfamily situation

is gaining the patience to wait out the stormy periods. As adults we often feel that because we have decided to go ahead with a new relationship everyone else will fall into line accordingly. Not so. For one thing, most stepchildren do not meet their stepparent-to-be until their natural parent has already made a fairly firm decision to marry. It is difficult for a child to take to the new adult with the kind of deep affection that takes time to develop; on the other hand, his or her natural parent may have already known the new person for six months or a year. Because of the initial suspicious phase between child and stepparent, which is only natural, many adults torture themselves with visions of family stress for years to come. One thing to be learned from the responses to this survey is that this is a false fear. Two things can happen: Either the children will take to their new step-relatives or they won't. If they do, the crisis is over. And it is equally over if they don't. The new family will settle into some sort of routine that is acceptable for all involved even if it is not full of love or affection. The worst thing that can happen is that one or both parents will keep trying to force the situation into a mold it won't fit into. Stepchildren cannot be forced to love you or vice versa, and if feelings of affection don't emerge, then that's just the way it is. The important thing is not to let concern about how the children feel disrupt the way the adults feel about each other so much that they divorce each other: Then the children will feel even worse, and they will have an entire new group of step-relatives to deal with. Many parents make the mistake of cosseting their children's happiness at the expense of their own, not realizing that it is the husband and wife's happiness that provides the mainstay of family life. If the parents' relationship is good, however many parents there are, the children will thrive. That is one element of family life that hasn't changed between the "traditional family" and the "future family."

Chapter Nine

Custody and Common Sense

No written law has ever been more binding than unwritten custom supported by popular opinion.

Carrie Chapman Catt

Consistency requires you to be as ignorant today as you were a year ago.

Bernard Berenson

There are few customs more resistant to change it seems than those involving the custody of children. Mothers still get 90 percent of the custody, and common sense and the welfare of the individuals involved take back seats to habit. Family structures have been changing, but the approach to custody has remained more or less static. Custody regulations and patterns no longer fit well with most people's situations. It is time to make long overdue changes in the way we handle this aspect of divorce.

One of the main attitudes that have to be altered before any changes can take place is thinking of the children of a marriage as possessions—spoils to be divided up at the time of the divorce along with the furniture, property, stocks and bonds, and the other material assets of the marriage. As long as we move the children around like pawns in the adult game of divorce, we will use them to suit whatever motives we may have for winning that game, from revenge and punishment on the one hand to rewards for "good behavior" on the other.

Some people may deny that that is the way we treat the "children of divorce," but why is it, then, that the custodial parent is permitted, if not encouraged, to use them as leverage against the noncustodial parent? How many mothers with custody have used their children as a way of punishing or rewarding their ex-husbands? Like carrots in front of a donkey, the children are dangled under the father's nose, but quickly withdrawn if he fails to live up to the standards of behavior set by the mother. There have been several cases in the last few years in which the custodial mother has gone to court to have the father's visiting privileges restricted because he either married or began living with another woman. In one case the mother insisted that she felt the moral climate in the father's home to be tainted by the presence of another woman and that she no longer wanted *her* children in such an environment. However, this did not stop the mother from enjoying a relationship with another man. It sounds rather more like a case of sour grapes than of actual danger of moral turpitude. A father does not have the same recourse if the mother remarries or lives with another man. He cannot go to court and refuse to make his child-support payments because the mother now has a live-in boyfriend and as a parent he disapproves of the situation.

Most courts insist that mothers should not be hindered by the law, or by their ex-husbands, from forming a new relationship after the marriage, whereas fathers are expected to put their obligations to their previous family, both financial and emotional, before any new relationships. The children's wishes are seldom considered.

CUSTODY AND THE LAW

As an example of how the law approaches the custody situation, we can again look at the Uniform Marriage and Divorce Act, which was taken into consideration in the provisions of the Uniform Child Custody Jurisdiction Act in matters of deciding custody. Even though this act has not been adopted in every state it is useful in describing the basic attitudes of the legal system toward custody cases because it codifies existing laws in most jurisdictions and is indicative of the prevailing attitude of judicial systems across the country on the issue of child custody.

Under Section 402 (Best Interests of the Child) the act says:

> The court shall determine custody in accordance with the best interests of the child. The court shall consider all relevant factors including:
>
> 1) the wishes of the child's parent or parents as to his custody
> 2) the wishes of the child as to his custodian
> 3) the interaction and interrelationship of the child with his parent or parents, siblings, and any other person who may significantly affect the child's best interests
> 4) the child's adjustment to his home, school and community and
> 5) the mental and physical health of all individuals involved.
>
> The court shall not consider conduct of a proposed custodian that *does not affect his relationship to the child.* [My italics.]

Having said all this the court still almost always awards custody to the mother. "The preference for the mother as custodian for young children when all things are equal for example is simply a shorthand method of expressing the best interests of the child and this section enjoins judges to decide custody cases according to that general standard."

Another reason why the mother usually gets custody is because she usually already *has* custody. With children as with things, possession appears to be nine points of the law. The logic goes something like this: Under Section 403 of the act (Temporary Orders) trials courts are encouraged to issue *temporary* custody orders *without a formal hearing* whenever possible. "In most cases it is expected the trial judges will award temporary custody to the existing custodian so as to minimize disruption to the child." Of course, since it is more often than not the father who moves out to accommodate his family he will not likely be the one to get temporary custody. Not suprisingly then, when permanent orders for custody are made, the judge usually looks at who has temporary custody and, unless something is very wrong, proceeds to award permanent custody to the same person in order not to disrupt the child.

If the father is not happy with this custody arrangement, he may, of course, protest and ask for a modification of the custody order, but under Section 409 of the act,

> No motion to modify a custody decree may be made earlier than one year after the date of the initial decree. If a motion for modification has been filed, whether or not it was granted, no subsequent motion may be filed within 2 years after disposition of the prior motion unless the court decides that there is reason to believe the child's present environment may endanger his physical health or mental development.

Even supposing that the father waits the year and then files an order for modification,

". . . the court shall not modify a prior custody decree unless it finds upon the basis of the facts that have arisen since the prior decree or that were unknown to the court at the time of the prior decree that a change has occurred in the circumstances of the child or his custodian and the modification is necessary to serve the best interests of the child. The court shall retain the custodian established by the prior decrees unless:

1) the custodian agrees to the modification
2) the child has been integrated into the family of the petitioner with the consent of the custodian
3) the child's present environment endangers his physical health.

In the comments following this section of the act it is noted that the intention of this section was to maximize *finality* of custody and thus assure continuity for the child. "Most experts who have spoken to the problems of post-divorce adjustment of children believe that ensuring the decree's finality is *more* important than determining which parent should be custodian." And further, "Any change in the child's environment may have an adverse effect *even if the non-custodial parent would better serve the child's interests.*" (My italics.) What has happened to the doctrine of "the best interests of the child" if a so-called *temporary* custody decision, made without a hearing, can be made permanent—even if change would be better for the child?

With laws such as this it seems that the approach of the courts toward the children of divorce is directed more toward deciding who "owns" the child than toward what is best for the child. But children are not hothouse plants. They can and do thrive in a multitude of environments, and they are probably better able to deal with changes in their lives than are the adults who make these custodial adjudications.

CREATING A "POWER PARENT"

By placing one parent's right of permanent ownership above
the individual child's interests (or those of the other parent)
the courts are setting up a situation in which one parent is
given tremendous power not only over the children but over
the other parent. This situation is lopsided at best, but if the
"Power Parent" has any negative feelings about how the
marriage ended or about the other parent, then the courts
are setting the stage for an on-going retributive war in which
the children are both weapons and casualties.

THE PLIGHT OF MOTHERS WHO DON'T WANT CUSTODY

Much has been said of mothers who get custody of their
children. Some think it is only right for the children, and
others think it has a lot to do with mothers' rights. Perhaps it
is time to devote some space to those mothers who get custody but who really don't want it and to the few mothers
who, in spite of the social and emotional repercussions involved, have given their custodial rights over to fathers or
other people. These women are just as much victims of
the motherhood myth as are the children who are forced to
give up one parent in favor of the other at the time of the
divorce.

Unfortunately our current attitudes about custody
more or less force these mothers to take their children or suffer the consequences. A little common sense could alleviate
this difficult situation for all concerned.

Just as there is widespread acceptance of the stereotype
of the irresponsible father who gives up his children with his
marriage, so too there is the less widespread but certainly

stronger feeling about the stereotype of the "unnatural mother"—the one who forsakes her true role in life by giving her children into the care and custody of their father. We are, as a society, convinced that such a woman is defective, if not totally rotten.

Women who have given up custody of their children either for the sake of the children's best interests, or because they want to devote more of their time to their careers, or because they recognize that they cannot cope with single parenthood, or because they know that the father is the more nurturant parent, are not lauded for a hard decision well made but instead suffer the social stigma of being called "unnatural."

There are more than 1 million absentee mothers in America, some by choice, some out of necessity, and it is time that we stopped branding them as being sinful and neglectful parents. The scarlet letter for the woman of the eighties stands not for adulteress it seems, but for absentee mother. But these women may be at the forefront of a new movement that really does consider the best interests of the children when arranging custody.

COULD YOU BE A CUSTODY CRIMINAL?

In 60 percent of the states, interference with a custody order is considered a felony. (Felony is a general term employed to distinguish certain high crimes from minor offenses known as misdemeanors.) Felony crimes are very serious business. So parental kidnapping of children in a custody dispute is treated with a lot more legal importance than it was a few years ago, when the state and federal enforcement agencies were loath to get involved in so-called domestic matters.

Though there are few statistics on who childnaps and why, there are estimated to be between 25,000 and 100,000 parental kidnappings a year. This trend in child stealing is directly related to three things: the rising divorce rate; the current custodial procedures, which are evidently not acceptable to many of today's divorcing parents; and a change in perception. Not many years ago it was impossible for parents to kidnap their own children because we just didn't think that a parent taking his or her own child was kidnapping.

The federal kidnapping statute, the Lindberg Act, specifically exempts parents from liability under its provisions. This exclusion was based on the idea that parents, even though they may be acting wrongly, are doing what they think best for the child. Certain states also have laws that exclude parents from liability in these cases. Where state laws do not specifically include exemption for parental abductions, courts have often been willing to hold that the parents' immunity is implied.

In one of the first cases to consider the issue, parental immunity was granted by the Pennsylvania Supreme Court (*Burns* vs. *Commonwealth*). This decision reflected an attitude that was, and still is in some states, common in cases of this nature—that is, child snatching by a parent is not seen as a violation of the personal right of the child but rather as an infringement of the property rights of the custodial parent in whose possession the child was supposed to remain. Abduction by a parent was, in fact, often condoned by the courts because it was seen as a natural extension of a parent's desire to be with the child.

Until recently, too, interstate custody laws often encouraged the kidnapping parent. It was quite simple to cross a state line and find a court in a different state that would refuse to give full effect to the custody decree of the original court and declare the petitioning parent to be the legal custodian of the child. This lack of uniformity among the states stemmed from three basic factors:

1. The United States Supreme Court has been unwilling to mandate that "full faith and credit" be given a sister state's custody decree.
2. State courts may exercise jurisdiction in custody disputes in a number of ways (i.e., courts may exercise jurisdiction based on the child's domicile, the child's presence, or the parent's domicile). So more than one court could assume jurisdiction in some cases.
3. Custody decrees are not final. They can be modified, and if the noncustodial parent can show changed circumstances in a different court then there is a good chance that the custody order will be changed because so much is left up to the discretion of the judge in deciding what is in the best interests of the child.

However, in an effort to bring more uniformity to this area of the law and to try to cut back the number of child-snatching cases, the Uniform Child Custody Jurisdiction Act (U.C.C.J.A.) was passed in 1977. The act changed the law of jurisdiction and stipulated that, in most instances, only one court would have continuing jurisdiction over any given custody case.

In 1980, the federal government jumped into the ring with the Parental Kidnapping Prevention Act. Considered primarily as a supplement to the U.C.C.J.A., its impact is as yet uncertain. Essentially this act is concerned with a national system for locating parents and children who have traveled from one jurisdiction to another while involved in such disputes, by the following means:

1. Promote cooperation between state courts to ensure that the state that would best decide the case maintains jurisdiction.
2. Promote cooperation between the states with respect to the providing of relevant information and assistance to other states involved in the same custody dispute.
3. Promote enforcement of custody decrees made in other states.
4. Discourage continuing interstate controversies over child custody.
5. Avoid jurisdictional disputes between state courts in matters that may result in shifting the child from state to state.
6. Deter abductions and removals of children to another state in order to obtain different custody awards.

The act even requires that states that do not adhere to the U.C.C.J.A. enforce custody regulations made in states that do and not modify such orders. If a parent abducts a child and seeks protection in one of the states or localities that does not use the U.C.C.J.A. (Massachusetts, New Mexico, Mississippi, South Carolina, West Virginia, Texas, the District of Columbia, Puerto Rico, and the Virgin Islands), then these states or localities will be under federal obligation to recognize and enforce the decree of the "home state" that took jurisdiction under U.C.C.J.A. regulations.

A previous custody determination can only be modified by the court of another state if the modifying state has jurisdiction, and if the original state no longer has jurisdiction or has refused to exercise that jurisdiction.

FEDERAL PARENT LOCATOR SERVICE

In order to help find an absent parent or child when his or her location is needed to make or enforce a child custody determination or to enforce a state or federal law dealing with the unlawful taking or restraint of a child, the Federal Parent Locator Service (FPLS) was instituted. It is not mandatory that states transmit requests to the FPLS, but any state may agree to aid the efforts of the FPLS by agreeing to receive requests to locate children and to pass such requests on to the FPLS. Parents themselves cannot apply directly to the FPLS for assistance, nor can their legal representative, but either a parent or his attorney can petition the court to request the FPLS to locate the absconding parent or missing child.

All of this, however, is only effective if the abducting parent wishes to follow legal procedure in gaining custody of the child. If he or she chooses to avoid this avenue, then the U.C.C.J.A. cannot help the legal parent regain custody of the child.

BEING IN CONTEMPT

If a parent violates the custody agreement either by removing the child from the custody of the custodial parent or by refusing the noncustodial parent the visitation rights that are part of the custody agreement, that parent is in contempt of court. Contempt of court is largely defined as "any act that is calculated to embarrass, hinder, or obstruct the court's administration of justice or that is calculated to lessen its authority or its dignity." A person found to be in contempt can be fined, subjected to forfeiture of a previously posted bond, and even imprisoned for refusal to comply with a court order. Generally speaking, fathers who do not pay their child support on time are in contempt of a court order, and that is why they can be fined or jailed.

Mothers who do not allow a required custody visit are also generally in contempt of a court order, but they have an edge in the situation. Because these mothers have custody most judges will think twice before finding them in contempt, as it then becomes an issue of who is going to look after the children while they are in jail or who will pay the fine for them.

The legal situation with respect to custody then has gone the gamut from one in which parents could legally kidnap their children to one in which it is, in some states, a felony. Surely the fact that the problem has escalated to this level must tell us that there is something wrong with our approach to custody. Elevating the removal of one's own children to the level of a serious crime is not going to solve the problem. It is rather a case of closing the barn door after the horse has bolted, because some harm will already have been done to the child, and also more and more parents who want custody at any cost will be driven underground. They may even be forced to flee internationally. Would it not be better to face the situation at the time of the divorce and make custodial arrangements fair to both parents so that we do not force one parent to such extremes? Surely we must consider other alternatives to the current approach to custody if for no other reason than that the children will not be at risk from a desperate absent parent.

CUSTODY ARRANGEMENTS

There are three basic types of custody arrangements: joint, split, and sole custody. There are also three basic kinds of joint custody, and there are a few other similar arrangements that may be combinations of these. Following are descriptions of the most common types of custody arrangements:

Sole Custody. The most popular form of custody at the present time, sole custody provides one parent with total control and legal responsibility for the child even to the point of deciding when, where, how often, and under what circumstances the child is permitted to see the other parent. The custodial parent is free to move the child across town or across the world, and the other parent has little or no recourse.

Joint Physical Custody. Both parents share the physical custody of the child, but only one has the full legal custody. This can be a bit awkward for the nonlegal parent who has no legal say in much of the child's life, although he is expected to share an equal responsibility for the child's behavior.

Joint Physical and Legal Custody. In this case both parents share the custody child equally and both are equally responsible.

Divided or Alternating Custody. Each parent has what is essentially sole custody for a period of the year. For instance, one parent may take the child during the summer and the other during the school year. But unless the parents also agree to make joint decisions about the child throughout the entire year, then the decision of the parent with whom the child is residing at a particular time will govern the situation at that time.

Split Custody. This was something that was more common among the respondents than joint custody. In this type of arrangement some of the children live with one parent and some with another, with appropriate visitation back and forth.

Joint Legal Custody.   In joint legal custody both parents retain and share the right to legal responsibility for the child though the child may actually live with only one of the parents. This means, for instance, that both can have access to his medical or educational records, both can make decisions about what schools he goes to or what religious training he gets, etc., and it also means that if he causes any trouble both parents are legally (and financially) responsible.

STATES WITH JOINT CUSTODY

Depending on whom you talk to about joint custody it is either the only solution to the current custody wars or the very last thing you would want to try. As with most things, however, it has its good side and its bad, and whether or not it works is largely dependent on the people who get involved in it and their commitment to good parenting.

As with many other aspects of family law, joint custody, because it is innovative and different in its approach, has not exactly been grabbed up by most courts as the answer to the custody problem. Many judges are against it because they see it as inherently unstable. But some states, such as California, are completely in favor of joint custody, as the following quote from the California Civil Code, Section 4600, demonstrates:

   a) The legislature finds and declares that it is the
        public policy of this state to assure minor chil-
        dren of frequent and continuing contact with
        both parents after the parents have separated

or dissolved the marriage and to encourage parents to share the rights and responsibilities of child-rearing in order to effect this policy.

In any proceeding where there is at issue the custody of a minor child, the court may, during the proceedings or at any time thereafter, make such an order for the custody of the child as may seem necessary or proper. In determining the persons to whom custody shall be awarded the court shall consider and give due weight to the nomination of a guardian of the person of the child by a parent under Article 1 (commencing with Section 1500) of Chapter 1 Part 2 of Division 4 of the Probate Code.

b) Custody should be awarded in the following order of preference according to the best interests of the child;

1) To *both* parents jointly pursuant to Section 4600.5 or to either parent. In making an order for custody to either parent, the court shall consider, among other factors, which parent is more likely to allow the child or children frequent and continuing contact with the non-custodial parent, and shall not prefer a parent as custodian because of that parent's sex. The court in its discretion may require the parents to submit to the court a plan for the implementation of the custody order.

Three other states actually have preferential joint custody legislation—Louisiana, Florida, and Nevada. In states where awards for joint custody are popular, there is some evidence of a reduction in sole father-custody awards; in California, for example, they went from a high of 9 percent in 1979 to less than 1 percent in 1984.

Other states with some form of joint custody legislation include Connecticut, Hawaii, Iowa, Kansas, Kentucky, Massachusetts, Michigan, Minnesota, Montana, New Hampshire, New Mexico, North Carolina, Ohio, Oregon, Texas, and Wisconsin. In addition, some states, even though they may not have actual legislation on the books, do tend to sympathize with and support joint custody applications. These include Alaska, Arizona, New Jersey, North Dakota, and Utah.

THE PROS AND CONS OF JOINT CUSTODY

Since there is so much disagreement about the benefits, if any, of the joint custody situation, perhaps it might be advantageous to examine both sides of the issue here in respect to the most important people involved, the children and the parents.

For the Children

The most obvious benefit of a joint custody arrangement for the children is that, having started out with two parents before the divorce, they get to continue in more or less that fashion after the divorce. We have already discussed the very necessary presence of fathers in the lives of their children, and joint custody is one way to make sure that that situation is maintained.

If children are legally in the custody of both parents, they are less likely to bear the brunt of their mother's anger or feel the sting of fatherly indifference that may result from many sole custody situations. Because both parents are essentially equal as parents under the law, just the way they were when they were married, neither one is in a position to use the children as a weapon against the other. Mother cannot refuse to let Dad see the kids because she is upset with him, and he is not in a position to refuse to "pay her," since he is now supporting them in his own home half of the time. At least this is the intent of joint custody. Its implementation, of course, depends a lot on the parents, but suffice it to say, if it works, the children are much better off. Many children report that they like being exposed to more than one life-style, and others note that joint custody allows them to get to know each of their parents better.

Among the disadvantages for the children is the possibility that they will not take well to living in two homes with two sets of rules and two different schedules. But young people may be better at adapting to new and different living arrangements than their parents.

For the Mother

It would seem that in today's world, when more and more women are concerned with their careers or going back to school, the possibility of joint custody would be embraced with open arms. After all, having custody half of the week, or two weeks a month, or whatever the arrangement may be, frees up a lot more time for other activities than having sole custody and responsibility all of the time. In addition, a woman can improve her standard of living by having more time to work and improve her self-esteem along with having time to enjoy her new independence. Also, she is not under the emotional strain of being totally responsible for her children's welfare and yet has the opportunity to spend a fair amount of time with them alone.

New studies have shown, too, that the more time fathers spend with their children and the more responsibility they feel for them on a daily basis, the more likely they are to pay their child support in full and on time. Why then are so many women so dead set against the idea of joint custody?

For a start, many feel it erodes their financial position. Because Dad has the children half the time, he will only pay her half the child support. Though that may seem quite just and reasonable, it also seems to upset a lot of so-called liberated mothers. Second, because they do not have sole custody, some women feel that they will be expected to become self-supporting since they now have the time to work. In addition, many women feel that their rights to their children are being eroded by allowing the father to have any legal rights at all. Last, such women might also lose control over their ex-husbands.

Whether or not joint custody may be in the children's best interests, a lot of mothers don't think it is in *their* best interests.

For the Father

The benefit of joint custody for the father is obvious. He gets to remain a legal parent as well as an emotional one. He can be assured that he will get to see his children when he is supposed to and that his ex-spouse cannot, in a fit of pique, decide otherwise. Nor can she remove them geographically far away or make decisions about their lives with which he does not agree. His financial burden is relieved somewhat, and his relationship with his children can be more natural than that of the visiting father who is forced to entertain his children every other Sunday. In other words, he can be a real dad.

For Both Parents

On the possibly negative side for both parents is the continued association with each other and possibly with each other's new spouses. This can require a lot of accommodating on all fronts, though it is worthwhile if it can be worked out. Also, for joint custody to work as it is intended, the parents must live near each other and consider the implications of moving to a new residence or to a new job if it means living farther away. The parents—all four of them—are therefore somewhat more restricted than they would be in other custody arrangements, but still, many find it a small price to pay for the well-being of their children.

PROFILE OF A JOINT CUSTODY PARENT

Who makes a good joint custody parent? Joint custody is certainly not right for everyone and some recent studies in the area have pointed out a few characteristics of the type of parent who generally makes a successful go of joint custody:

1. Parents who choose joint custody in the first place tend to be relatively more affluent and well educated and to give parenting a very high priority on their list.
2. They generally make the decision for joint custody themselves rather than having it imposed on them by a court of law.
3. As a group, they tend to have high levels of maturity and flexibility and are able to handle the complexities of finances and scheduling necessary for successful shared parenting.
4. The last and perhaps most important ingredient for successful joint custody is that both

parents must be able and willing to put aside
their negative feelings, if any, for each other
and consider instead what is best for the children.

A majority of parents involved in a shared parenting situation report a more positive attitude toward their ex-spouse
as a result of the joint custody arrangement. This is not to
say that shared parenting leads to a shared living arrangement between ex-spouses. Most joint custody parents limit
their good feelings about each other only to matters relating
to the children.

In cases in this study where stepparents were involved,
the new partners were seen to have a positive effect on the
children. However, they were not viewed by the children as
parent substitutes (since the real thing was still available)
but rather as friends. The effect of one or both parents having a new relationship did not seem to adversely affect the
shared parenting agreement in any negative way. It seems
that a joint custody arrangement might even take some of
the pressures off the parents' new relationships.

HOW TO GO ABOUT JOINT CUSTODY

There is no doubt that significant advantages exist for those
in a joint custody situation, though one tends to think perhaps that people who make such a situation work would
probably be reasonable enough as individuals to make any
custody situation work well. However, for those interested in
seeing what it takes to make such an agreement, the guide-
lines are presented below.

In over 80 percent of joint custody households, the idea
was suggested initially by one of the parents, not by a lawyer
or other professional. It is therefore a very personal decision

that can be adapted to suit the particular needs of the family involved. Whatever is convenient is probably best, whether that includes split weeks, every other week, or even every other day. Joint custody does not mean that both parents have to make a fifty/fifty split of the children's time. It can, in fact, be any ratio that fits the particular family. In 50 percent of the joint custody cases in a recent study, the parents shared equal time with the children, but in 30 percent of the cases they split their time seventy-five/twenty-five, with the children spending the school week with one parent and the weekends with the other. Others who lived farther apart went so far as splitting the year—with vacations spent with one parent and school weeks with the other. But no matter what the schedule, both parents had equal legal rights and responsibility for their children.

THE JOINT CUSTODY AGREEMENT

It is a good idea, once the parents have agreed to have joint custody, to put the arrangement in writing. That way, the court will be more willing to listen to a proposal of joint custody (remember, in most states custody is still decided at the discretion of the judge), and also both the mother and father will know what the ground rules are if something comes up in the future.

A good joint custody agreement should include the following elements:

1. A basic Statement of Intent: Here the parents would include their names and their children's names and the fact that they both intend to participate in a joint custody process.
2. An acknowledgment of an agreement to share custody as set out in the rest of the document

should follow the Statement of Intent. This section should include a written schedule for both school weeks and holidays and some schedule to cover special occasions such as Christmas, birthdays, etc.

3. There should be a clear definition of the parents' responsibilities with reference to such things as support (what percentage each parent will pay—remember joint custody does not have to mean equal support), medical insurance, extraordinary purchases, tuition, clothing, etc.

4. Each parent should agree to co-operate with the other about picking up and dropping off the child if that is necessary, not suddenly changing plans at the last minute, and not moving without discussing it with the other parent. Common courtesy is the rule here. In addition, there should be some mention of each parent's responsibility to the other parent. For instance, in case of an emergency they could agree to contact the other parent right away.

5. The parents should agree on who will claim the tax deduction for the child.

6. Also, the parents should agree on who will hold life insurance for the child, who will make the child beneficiary, and how much the policies will be.

7. The parents should consider what will happen in the case of the death of one or both parents.

8. The parents should decide what will happen in the event that one or both of them remarry and have other children.

9. They might also want to agree at this time on how to solve future disagreements, such as

choosing mediation rather than immediately going back to court.

Basically anything the parents can think of in terms of the child's ultimate needs and his or her own needs can be included. As you can see, each joint custody agreement can be very specific and very individual, much like a marriage contract. If done with sufficient thought and consideration, such contracts can be not only legally binding but, more important, can also save a lot of headaches later on.

The one major problem with such agreements is that they make some adults feel restricted in terms of what they can do with their lives. Under a tightly written joint custody agreement, there is not much room for spontaneity. It would be difficult, for instance, to have a very detailed agreement with respect to time and place, if your job required you to be able to pick up and go at a moment's notice or even if you had a job where overtime was frequently required, unless the other spouse was very understanding and co-operative. However, many people can and do make such agreements work, and generally speaking, if you have been able to fit children into your life before the divorce, you should be able to fit a tailor-made joint custody agreement into it afterward.

Though joint custody or its offshoots will not work for every family, it does work for some. What would work better for everybody is if the adults involved would put aside their own motives for custody, their game-playing and their attempts to control others through their children, and just ask themselves one question: "What would be the best custody situation for the children?"

Let us hope that they would get a truthful answer, which would go a long way to putting an end to today's "custody wars" and putting the common sense back into custody.

Chapter Ten

Divorce–A New Beginning

When I can no longer bear to think of the victims of broken homes, I begin to think of the victims of intact ones.
Peter De Vries

The happiest time of anyone's life is just after the first divorce.
John Kenneth Galbraith

The act of divorce has become more and more simple over the last few years. Much of the finger pointing and scapegoating that marked the long drawn-out divorces of the past has thankfully been alleviated, if not completely removed, by a move toward no-fault divorce in many states. Divorce, in fact, is well on its way to becoming an acceptable, if expensive, legal procedure. What has not changed, however, is the way we as a society still feel about divorce.

Most people perceive divorce to be a failure of the individuals involved in the marriage. The individuals themselves usually look for someone or something to blame and often end up laying that blame incorrectly on themselves. They carry a sack full of guilt and self-recrimination with them for years, sometimes ruining future relationships because of their assumed "failure" at the first marriage.

But why do we persist in the idea that divorce is "The End" of everything? One of the reasons is that divorce is the logical antithesis to marriage, and we have learned to regard marriage—at least the first marriage—as "The Great Beginning." But every change of state is the end of one period and the beginning of another. Divorce is the end of a marriage, but marriage is also the end of life as a single person. Divorce is restoring the individuals who have lived for a time as a couple back to their earlier state, as individuals.

What we should really be focusing on is not divorce as the end and marriage as the beginning but rather on each as a process of change. If we could perceive divorce the way we perceive marriage, as a change of circumstances and not a finality from which we are never to recover, we could save ourselves and our children a lot of unhappiness and pain.

DIVORCE IN THE LONG TERM

It is sometimes difficult to say whether studies that monitor the effects of divorce on children, studies that have become a popular area of research in the last few decades, create popular opinion or reflect it. Certainly most of the studies on children and divorce showed very negative effects, as we discussed at the beginning of this book.

Over the years our attitudes about children and divorce have changed in direct relation to the increased importance of children in the family, something which is itself directly related to the increasing vociferousness of women in society as a whole. The more emphasis we have placed on the child as the focal point of family life, the more negative we have decided are the effects of divorce on that child. Back in the days when children were to be "seen but not heard," no one really cared very much how children reacted if their parents separated, because the marriage was the business solely of the adults involved and the children were expected to adjust to whatever came their way. But now our child-kings must be protected from divorce and its aftermaths at all costs.

As an example of how faddish opinions about the child in relation to the divorce process can be, consider that just over a decade ago, Anna Freud, Joseph Goldstein, and Albert Solnin produced their work entitled *Beyond the Best Interests of the Child,* in which they recommended that a child of divorce should be in the custody of one parent and one parent only, either the mother or the father. Nowadays, many experts recommend prolonged and frequent contact with both parents, whether through joint custody or frequent visitation.

When it comes to research into the effects of divorce on children it appears that, as with divorce itself, a lot depends on how you look at it and what you are looking for. All research reflects the natural bias of the times. That is why, with the ever increasing divorce rate forcing more people to re-examine their feelings about divorce and children, there is now a definite swing away from the idea that divorce is traumatic and that any negative effects are long-lasting. After all, when what was once considered to be abnormal becomes increasingly more normal, then our perceptions of the situation must change.

The National Institute of Mental Health research effort that supported and co-ordinated studies from around the country proved, according to Nicholas Zill, President of Child Trends Inc. in Washington, "that a lot of children get through divorce without a lot of long-term problems." Preliminary findings of the studies have concluded that, although divorce can be painful or discomforting to children at the time, the children of divorce don't grow up much differently from children of intact homes.

Among the findings of this extensive report were:

1. Children under twelve who live with divorced mothers actually do better on achievement tests and have fewer school problems than those from intact homes because divorced parents pay more attention to their children and make a greater effort to get involved in every facet of their lives, including school.
2. Children aged twelve to sixteen who live in homes where married parents argue frequently are more likely to be antisocial, to lie, and to bully other children than are those who live with divorced parents.
3. Adults whose parents are divorced are arrested half as often as adults from intact homes.
4. Adults from divorced homes are more careful about whom they choose to marry than adults from intact homes. They also tend to be more cautious in many other aspects of life and to work harder.

The study done by Project Teen Canada noted that the significance of the separation and divorce for children is directly related to the quality of home life before the divorce. Children who have experienced much stress in their so-called intact homes would therefore be expected to have a more difficult time with the divorce process. The study also indicated that a key factor in how well children handled the divorce was the mental health of the parent with custody, and that parents with custody who were anxious or depressed were likely to contact social agencies regarding the mental health of their *children*. This may be the reason so many previous studies on the children of divorce have found those children to be traumatized. If anxious and depressed parents project their feelings onto their children or if the children had a particularly bad time at the end of the marriage, it is more than likely that the parents will have a propensity to suggest that their children participate in studies on the children of divorce. The results of such studies would prove to be negative. However, they would not reflect the situation of the population in general but only the subsection that was having a problem with divorce.

The NIMH report, however, may prove to be the light at the end of the tunnel for the children of divorce and their parents. It is the first large-scale study to suggest that divorce is not the harmful event that forever tarnishes the lives of all the children involved. The overall results of the study suggest that it is not the divorce but the events and circumstances subsequent to it that can do the real damage. This finding is something that respondents definitely stand behind, as we can see in their comments on the aftermath of divorce in their own lives and how they feel it affected them.

THE CHILDREN OF WISDOM

The saying "Nothing teaches like experience" is very true when it comes to going through a divorce, good or bad, for there is something to be learned from it either way. Those who took the time to answer the questionnaire proved this saying very well. Some of them had a difficult time with their parents' divorce. Others did not. But, in spite of their own personal experiences, most realized that the divorce was at the very least making the best of a bad situation and that maintaining the marriage would have been an error, far in excess of the discomfort that may have been caused by the divorce. On top of that, most learned a good deal about human relationships and how they work. Their rational approach and, in some cases, their wisdom were surprising considering their ages. This ability to comprehend and to adjust is not something that adults in general appear to expect from children going through their parents' divorce. Perhaps if we want to re-educate ourselves to another perception of divorce we had better listen to what the children say.

In answer to the question, "How do you feel about divorce in general?" 65 percent of the respondents had generally positive feelings, 28 percent generally negative feelings, and 7 percent were neither negative nor positive. Whatever their feelings, their answers were well thought out and surprisingly mature considering how young many of them were. For this reason, the ages have been included following their comments given in answer to this question.

It is also interesting to note that, for the most part, they see divorce as a solution that should only be arrived at after every other avenue has been exhausted. This attitude, then, is not convergent with the beliefs of many critics of divorce who feel that children of divorced parents will seek the easy way out of marriage at the first sign of a problem because they have observed the role of divorce in their parents' troubled marriage. In fact, if anything, the opposite is true, and these people have much more conservative attitudes toward both marriage and divorce than their parents.

> *"Divorce sometimes is the only answer after much trying, counseling, etc. So much more is now known about how to help a child get through a divorce that I don't think, if it is handled properly by those involved, there is any need for it to be traumatic." (age 51)*

> *"I think divorce is O.K. I don't think a couple should force themselves to stay together for the benefit of others, although I think they could avoid divorce if they were more certain before they married." (age 17)*

"I think it's a bad example to show children that the easiest way to solve a problem is to run away from it and not really try and work it out. But if you do try and it still doesn't work, then what else can you do?" (age 18)

"Sometimes you have to do what is necessary." (age 21)

"There have been some specific hurts from it, but life would have been much more worse if we had just gone on as before." (age 19)

"If all else fails, it is an important alternative to living together and being unhappy." (age 31)

"I think it was the best thing for everyone involved. Divorce is fine with me as long as it is not spiteful and hurtful." (age 22)

"I think divorce can be a very good thing, but a lot depends on how it is handled." (age 20)

"Sometimes it happens. No one 'wants' to get divorced, but if things are bad in the marriage then that is the answer." (age 36)

"If you can't be happy with the person you are married to, then you should get divorced." (age 26)

"I think we would all like to think that marriage can be permanent, but sometimes people just grow apart and then divorce is a viable solution." (age 23)

"I believe in it sincerely. Some marriages should never have been in the first place—my parents', for instance—and divorce was just correcting the situation." (age 54)

"I'm all for it if both parties agree that it is what's best for them. After all it is their lives and it's really nobody else's business." (age 21)

"As the saying goes, 'I'd rather come from a broken home than live in one.' "(age 18)

Divorce does not seem to be so much "an end" for these children as a logical and completely necessary alternative to a marriage that no longer makes the people in it happy. Proof of this attitude was offered by the answers to the question, "Would you rather your parents had stayed together until you left home?" Note, the option here was not for the parents to stay together permanently, something that, in most cases, the children would have realized was impossible, but simply for them to stay until the children were grown and on their own.

The answers, if we are to believe the myth of the overwhelming trauma of divorce, should have been a very definite "Yes," because no child wants to see himself or herself placed in a painful situation if there is an alternative. As it turns out, the opposite was true. In fact, in answer to this question 76 percent of the respondents said, "No," they would not have preferred that their parents had stayed together. Of the remainder, 21 percent said, "Yes," and 3 percent did not know.

"No! I think it was terrible for them to have stayed together as long as they did in the first place. It only made them more miserable and everyone else too."

"I don't think so. They would have kept living a lie had they stayed together and it was better in the long run for everyone that they got divorced."

"I would rather they had loved each other enough to want to stay together, but I certainly didn't want them to stay together under the same circumstances."

"No. If they had divorced earlier it would have been better not only for my mother but for me too, because things would not have degenerated to the level they finally did before the divorce. There might have been something left to salvage."

"I would have liked them to stay together to help prevent my feelings of being a 'limbo' child, but I realize there's no guarantee I wouldn't have had these feelings anyway if they had stayed together."

"No. I don't think they would have been happy. Besides, I think that children adjust much easier than adults so I'm glad they did it when they did and not when I was older."

"No way! *I would have been a basket case."*

"It didn't really matter. It would have hurt me just as much but in a different way if they had stayed together."

"The tension and fighting were unbearable. They could not have stayed married. It would have been awful for everyone."

"I think it would have been very selfish of me to put what I wanted at the moment before what was best for them and for me too in the long run."

"No. Their happiness was too important to me."

"No. Together, they made terrible parents. Apart, they're O.K."

Not only did the respondents approach the situation with a very common-sense attitude, but their lack of selfishness was also surprisingly apparent, as was their sense of self-preservation. Most of them did not resort to the fantasy that everything would have been fine if only their parents had stayed together (an idea with which adults often like to dally).

CAN DIVORCE BE CATCHING?

Some people fear that, like a virus, divorce could cut a swath through the fabric of American society with results that could be devastating to family life as we know it. Divorce, they feel, could be catching. They shy away from friends who are going through the withdrawal pains of a terminated marriage because they are afraid that somehow it may happen to them too. Many also believe that those in the highest possible risk group for catching "The Divorce Bug" are those who have been most closely associated with a divorce—the children. They believe that, having observed their parents solving marital strife with a trip to the divorce court, they too will seek out the permanent "easy" cure if their own marriage sickens.

In answer to the question, "Would you ever consider getting divorced?" 67 percent of the respondents said "yes," 29 percent said "no," and the rest did not know. However, it should be noted that they generally saw divorce as the very last step in the process of solving the problem of an unhappy marriage, and not something to be taken at all lightly. Because these people have seen the machinations of a divorce close up, they are more familiar with it and more likely to consider it an alternative if the situation demands it than people who haven't. They are not going to be more likely to use it as the first solution to the problem because they, of all people, know how difficult a divorce can be.

> *"Divorce is a real possibility. If my marriage got to the point where I was desperately unhappy, of course I would consider getting divorced."*

> *"I certainly couldn't rule it out, but I would have to get married first and that is not something I plan at the moment."*

> *"Rather than taking mental or physical abuse of course I would get a divorce. I saw what happened to my mother and I don't want the same to happen to me, so I would get out before things got that bad."*

> *"I have been divorced once, but now I'm trying very hard to make my second marriage last so it won't happen again."*

> *"Yes, if I was abused or married to a lazy bum I couldn't communicate with, or if I fell out of love. I'd go to counseling first, though."*

> *"I was divorced after four miserable years. Now, finally, I am happy."*

> *"For the time being I am not even considering getting married."*

> *"I think I would try to think very carefully about who I was marrying first so that I wouldn't need to get divorced, but if I was very unhappy, I suppose I would consider it."*

> *"If the relationship got extremely bad, unbearable, with no hope of overcoming the problems, then I would get a divorce."*

> *"I suppose those whose parents are divorced are supposed to say 'yes,' they would because they have been through it and know*

how it works, but I don't know. I should hope that I would have taken enough time and consideration when choosing my spouse to avoid divorce. But I am not afraid of it."

Divorce is never a lightly chosen solution to a crumbling marriage, even for children of divorce. One of the positive effects of having a divorce in the family, though, seems to be that it makes one *more* careful when choosing a partner, not less.

When asked if it should be made easier or more difficult for people to get divorced in the future, the answers were somewhat surprising. Thirty-eight percent said divorce should be made easier to get, 24 percent said it should be more difficult, 15 percent said it should be about the same, and 23 percent answered the question by saying that we should try a dose of preventive medicine by making a marriage license more difficult to get.

"Easier. Definitely. If you don't hate the spouse before the divorce you sure do afterward. The lawyers prey upon people emotionally, legally, and financially."

"It's hard enough to go through the break-up of a relationship without having to go through all the legal nonsense, not to mention the expense."

"It should be made more difficult to get divorced. That would force couples to get along. If the divorce laws were harder, then people would think twice before getting married too."

"I don't think it should be made easier or more difficult. But people should be encouraged to try to work it out before getting a divorce by going to counseling."

"I don't think it should be made easier because then people are going to get married without being sure of the person they marry.

Besides, it only takes a couple of years if you really want a divorce at the moment."

"Much easier. By the time the couple gets to the point where they want to take legal action they are sure of their incompatibility, and the legal hassles only add to the strife."

"Never mind about divorce. It's marriage that should be made more difficult so that people don't need to get divorced."

"We should change our attitude about divorce and stop trying to put the blame all on one person. It isn't always one person's fault when a marriage comes apart."

"It really should be up to the couple."

"Easier because then all the bad feelings wouldn't get worse, and then the children wouldn't be dragged back and forth so much."

"It should be made easier. We have to understand that sometimes people just don't get along with each other any more."

"If it was easier, there would be less hassle and less emotional upheaval for everyone, especially the children."

"I think it should be made easier. Either that or make getting married equally as difficult."

HOW THE CHILDREN WOULD DO IT BETTER

It appears that the respondents have a very poor opinion of the way we handle divorce and marriage in this society. Since they have some inside knowledge of the experience, they were asked, "How do you think your parents could have handled the divorce situation differently?" and "How would you have handled the situation if it had been your divorce?"

The majority of Solomon's Children felt their parents could have done a better job of getting divorced. This is an important consideration because all along we have been blaming the act itself when perhaps we should have been pointing a finger at those who were involved in it. It may very well be that the way we divorce and not the fact that we get divorced lies at the root of many of our own negative feelings about the experience and its effects on our children.

In this study 80 percent of the respondents said they thought their parents could have handled things differently. In addition, 82 percent said that if it had been their divorce they would not have done things in the same way. This would indicate that while children of divorced families may consider divorce as a more viable possibility than other children, they also have learned by observation how *not* to divorce and therefore can save themselves and their own children a lot of discomfort if they do decide to get divorced.

"They could have talked to us about it. If it had been me, I would have tried counseling first."

"I think they handled it very well. I don't think I could have done any better."

"I wish they had come and told us about it together instead of leaving it for somebody else to do. It seemed like such a foreign thing then."

"They should have talked to us more, and I think we should have gone to a therapist. If it had been me though, I would have gotten out much sooner."

"I wish they had done it sooner. Their marriage was in pieces for years, and they kept hanging on, hoping it would somehow get better when it was obvious that it never would. I would have got it over with much sooner."

"They should have been more open about the causes and effects so that we understood better why it was happening. And they should have refrained from fighting in front of the children. That's what I would hope I would do."

"I think they should have separated before they did. I know they stayed together mostly for the sake of my sister and me, but we all knew they were having problems and that it was getting worse. It was really very hard to have to pretend that it was one big loving family when it wasn't. I don't think I would have waited so long, and I know that I wouldn't have contested the divorce the way my mother did."

"Dad could have put some more effort into trying to work things out, but I guess since he really wanted the divorce it wouldn't have made any difference. Mom could have tried to be more understanding. If a divorce was what my husband wanted and we had really tried everything else but there was no way, then I would give myself some time, get mad, get sad, and then get on with my life."

"It would have been much more civilized if only they had done it earlier. That is what I would do."

"I wish they had talked to me more and been more concerned with how I felt. As a mother I would not put my kids in the middle but would let them know that we both still loved them in spite of the divorce."

"They should have been more friendly to each other. I would not say the things they said in front of the children."

"I think they should have let us choose who to live with. I would let my children choose."

"They should have been more reasonable with each other and with us. At no point during this time do I remember any effort to make calm, mature communication. As for me, I would have sought professional help before things got that bad, and I would never have asked my children to take sides."

"My father could have exercised more maturity and ignored the influence of his mother. If it were 1958 and I'd been in my mother's position, I guess I'd have given in too. Social forces against her were powerful then. But if it were now, I'd tell him to shove his adultery charge and fight him tooth and nail for custody."

"They could have explained what was happening and not run each other down so, and, especially, Mom should have let me have a relationship with my father. I would have tried to be more adult about the whole thing, worked out a visitation schedule, and never criticized the other parent in front of the children."

In spite of the fact that Solomon's Children learned a lot about how not to get divorced from first-hand experience, 83 percent said that they understood better now why their parents got divorced (and perhaps why they handled it so badly), 7 percent said they understood perfectly well at the time of the divorce but 10 percent said they still didn't really understand what happened. Communication, it would seem, is one of the things that is most lacking between divorcing parents and their children. Perhaps if we were not so afraid to confront the idea of divorce and perhaps could even look upon it more positively, the issue of communication would resolve itself.

"I understand the whole thing 100 percent better now."

"*Yes. I understand now that when one person stops loving the other there is no good reason to stay married.*"

"*I can see their situation very clearly now, and I think they did what was right.*"

"*Yes. They were both very immature people who were very dependent personalities. Neither one offered the other any support.*"

"*Yes. Mom was much too young to get married. She had never lived on her own, had had no time to grow up. To get married because you are pregnant is never a good idea.*"

"*The marriage was doomed from the start. They were both too selfish.*"

"*I can analyze the situation better now that I have had a relationship of my own that didn't work out, and I can see what happened to theirs.*"

"*I understood it at the time. It was completely straightforward. They hid nothing from us.*"

"*I understand better now mostly because I've gotten to know my dad and he's explained a lot I didn't know before.*"

"*I understood better as I got older. Young children really cannot comprehend the idea of love and marriage and what it entails for those who are involved. They are only concerned with their feelings and have not yet learned to consider the feelings of others.*"

"*Facts have been disclosed to me that have made things clearer as I got older and was able to understand them.*"

"*Maturity helps, and time. I think they understand what happened better now as well as me.*"

Time and maturity do, it seems, make a difference in how children perceive their parents' divorce, and yet so many parents base their own perceptions of divorce on the memory of the face of an anxious four-year-old. Whenever we talk about the effects of divorce on children it is always that scared little face that is conjured up, but this is not a fair representation of how all children feel about the divorce of their parents. That short period of confusion and stress doesn't last, unless we encourage it to last. The trouble is, we often do just that by letting our guilt get the better of us or because it ultimately suits our own ends—such as revenge.

But while we are busy struggling with our emotional burdens of divorce, whether they are meant to cause self-inflicted or other-inflicted pain, the children who are the supposed reason for our self-castigation are busy getting on with their lives and putting the divorce behind them. If that were not the case, then surely the children of divorce would have a very wary and unsatisfying relationship with their parents in later years.

From the following statistics you will notice how intact the divorced parent-child relationship is compared to how uncivilized and often hurtful is the relationship between ex-spouses, who cannot or choose not to put the past behind them. I think these figures indicate that, of the closely involved parties, the children are the ones who manage to handle the divorce best of all.

Overall, 74 percent of the respondents said they had a good relationship with at least one of their parents years after the divorce. Of that 74 percent, 35 percent said their relationship was good with both parents, 28 percent said it was good with just their mother, and 38 percent said their relationship was good with just their father. Of those who did not enjoy a good relationship, 64 percent said that their relationship with their mother was bad and 36 percent said the same of their relationship with their father. In addition to their relationships with their parents, 68 percent said they were on good terms with their stepparents, 24 percent said they weren't, and 9 percent said they had ambiguous feelings about their stepparents.

> *"I'm really very close to my father because we live in the same town, but it is really good with both of them."*

> *"My relationship is really good with both of them even though over the years it has become apparent that my dad has some serious mental problems. But I'm all he has, and even if I wasn't I would love him anyway."*

> *"My relationship with my parents is very mature and strong."*

> *"My mother and I have remained very close even though we live in different cities. I haven't seen my dad for seven years."*

> *"My mother is one of my best friends and I am getting to know my father better. So far, I like what I see. His second wife is very special to me as well."*

> *"I haven't seen my mother in twenty years. She says she hates me and that I only want to hurt her more. But my father was always there for me."*

> *"I'm pretty much at ease with my father now, though we don't always see eye to eye on everything. But I love him very much and look up to him. As for my stepmother, we don't get along very well, and I'm not really sure whose fault that is."*

> *"In some ways I am closer to both of them because of the divorce. I talk a lot with my mom, and because they are divorced I make an effort to talk and write to my dad often. I don't think I would try this hard if they were still married."*

"I love my mother and am still trying to forgive her imperfections. I love my father and miss him very much."

"My dad and I have a wonderful relationship. He is one of my very best friends. I moved into my own apartment last year, and my relationship with my mother is still strained because she can't seem to accept my growing up. But I think things are improving gradually. I have a really good relationship with my stepmother but not with my stepfather, which is the real reason I moved out."

"Things are distant but friendly with Dad and rather superficial with Mother—just like when they were married."

"Things are great. I love them all."

Children don't stop liking or loving their parents just because they get divorced, although, as we have seen, they may change their opinions about parents who don't handle the divorce well. Perhaps that is because parents are supposed to be the standards by which we judge ourselves, and many children of divorce don't like to think of themselves acting the way they have seen their parents act. But, in a way, they are fortunate because they often get to see more of the real people behind the parental facade than do most children.

THE TRUTH ABOUT THE CONSEQUENCES

If you perceive something as having only negative connotations, then it will have them. For many people in the past, adults and children alike, divorce has been a self-fulfilling prophecy. No good could come of it, that was what we were taught, and anybody who went through it had to suffer and be marked for life by the experience.

But while all these bad opinions about divorce were being aired, there were a lot of children in America who had divorcing parents and who were managing just fine, thank you. If they were having a few problems, it was more likely the result of how other people were acting and feeling about divorce than of how they themselves were feeling.

We asked the question, "What was the hardest thing for you to deal with re your parents' divorce?" Fifty-six percent of the respondents said that other people and their responses to the situation were the hardest thing to deal with.

"The hardest thing was not having my mom around because then I had to do the housework."

"I think the hardest thing was not knowing my father well."

"At first it was embarrassment, but later it was having no one to share my mother's problems with so that I had to look after her by myself."

"I didn't like the way people singled me out for special attention. I didn't like the pity."

"It was hard not thinking of us as a family any more and having to share special occasions with other people."

"Having the familiar patterns of my life altered. I guess change is always difficult, but then you do adjust after a while and sometimes things are actually better."

"I hated the ping-pong effect of going back and forth between two houses."

"I felt so unloved. Nobody would listen to me or pay attention to me. It was like my feelings weren't important."

"It was hard to get used to the fact that moms and dads didn't always live together forever."

"I hated the constant backbiting. It went on for years. In fact it still is."

"I was afraid for a while that the same thing would happen to me."

"I found it hard to get used to my parent's sexuality, which was more openly expressed after the divorce."

"I didn't like seeing my mother unhappy and I missed my dad."

For the 44 percent who felt that their brush with the negative side of divorce was more self-related, the answers went like this:

"I missed the guidance most of all. I think we both got very spoiled because of the divorce and did not learn good values."

"I felt like I lost total control of my world. It hurt my self-confidence because I felt rejected by both of them."

"Both my parents wanted custody and so were constantly pulling me back and forth. It was as though their need to hurt each other was more important than what was happening to me."

"I have always lived with the desire to know what I and my family would have been like if the divorce had not been necessary."

"I think it colored my outlook on marriage."

"I started using drugs and being promiscuous because I wanted their attention."

> *"I did not grow up with my dad, and so I had a hard time relating to men and feel very nervous around them."*

Most of these comments indicate that it is the way the divorce is dealt with by the couple that can have negative effects on the children involved and not the fact that they got divorced. However, inasmuch as some people don't divorce very well, there are still some who do, and there are also some very positive consequences of divorce as far as the children are concerned.

Of those who answered the question, "What was the best thing that happened to you as a result of your parents' divorce?" 89 percent said something good happened as a direct result of the divorce. Only 11 percent said that nothing good came out of the divorce. Of those who reported a positive result, 45 percent said it made them a better person, 26 percent said it gave them a better family life, 12 percent said it gave them a better life, and 6 percent said it made others happier.

> *"I got to have my stepfather's parents as grandparents. They were wonderful people."*

> *"The constant tension in my home was finally released."*

> *"I grew up more quickly and became very independent and self-sufficient at a younger age."*

> *"I was very careful who I chose to marry. I watched successful marriages and tried to emulate them. Above all, I learned how important it is to communicate with each other, and after thirty-three years it still works!"*

> *"It made me more mature. I know the world doesn't have to come to an end and that I can handle any situation that comes my way. I learned how to get to the point."*

"*I found a new father and an aunt who both have lots of love in them.*"

"*It made my move away from home much easier as I didn't feel that I should stick around and try and help them sort things out.*"

"*It made my father and mother both a lot happier.*"

"*My life is so much more stable now.*"

"*I got to experience more different life-styles and people, and that has made me much more broad-minded.*"

"*I got to know both my parents better—as people.*"

"*I got financial support from the government to go to high school and to university which I wouldn't have been able to do otherwise.*"

"*I gained an ability to examine my inner self and know what I need. It has made my own marriage stronger.*"

"*I developed strength and independence at an early age and learned to analyze situations and people and to communicate my feelings better.*"

"*I feel that because of my young age I by-passed any possible trauma. I feel it was a good thing knowing my parents as I do and that because of the divorce I was able to get closer to both of them without having the tension of their marriage interfere.*"

"*I know that I would have been a very screwed up person if I had grown up with father's influence. As it is, I have a pretty healthy self-image.*"

"I got to know more about reality. I realized that my life and everyone in it wasn't always going to be the way I wanted it. I think their divorce matured me and made me more responsible as a person."

"Because of my parents' divorce I was able to grow and learn as a person. I don't think I would be the man I am today if they had stayed together."

"Because of their divorce I learned a lot about relationships and how they should work. I don't think I will be likely to make the same mistakes in my life that they made."

The consequences of divorce for the children, then, are often part of a popular misperception rather than reality. Children are wonderful, resilient people who can and do handle life quite well, even when it gets difficult. Seeing divorce through their eyes has to make us wonder if we shouldn't adjust our attitudes toward this process. It is time we stopped being so hypocritical and gave some thought to how our divorce behavior affects the children, instead of using them as a way to get at each other and to serve our own ends while loudly proclaiming otherwise. If divorce has traumatized some children, it is because their parents cared more about themselves than about what was really in the best interests of their children.

Divorce is not going to go away. Why then not make it easier on both the parents and the children, instead of condoning a system that pits each against the other? Why not look at divorce as being a means of correcting unhappiness, instead of creating it? A good divorce is better than a bad marriage for everyone concerned.

The time has come when we should let people arrange their family life according to what is good for them today and not what was acceptable in the past. There is nothing wrong with people wanting to be happy in a marriage even if it is not the marriage they started out with. There is nothing wrong with fathers wanting to have custody of their children and have an equal right to participate in their lives. There is nothing wrong with mothers who don't want the pressures of constant custody. And there is nothing wrong with Solomon's Children that a more positive attitude toward divorce and a new approach to custody would not cure.

References

BOOKS AND PERIODICALS

Atkin, Edith, and Estelle Rubin. *Part-Time Father*. New York: Vanguard Press, 1976.

Badinter, Elisabeth. *Mother Love: Myth and Reality*. New York: Macmillan, 1981.

Berman, Claire. *Making It as a Stepparent*. New York: Bantam Books, 1981.

Bureau of the Census (U.S. Dept. of Commerce). *Statistical Abstract of the United States, 1984*, 104th ed. Washington, D.C.: 1984.

Chafe, William H. *The American Woman*. New York: Oxford University Press, 1972.

Franks, Maurice R. *A Lawyer Reveals: How to Avoid Alimony.* New York: E.P. Dutton, 1975.

Friedan, Betty. *The Feminine Mystique*, 20th anniv. ed. New York: Laurel Books, 1983.

Gardner, Richard A. *The Parents Book About Divorce.* New York: Bantam Books, 1980.

————.*The Boys and Girls Book About Step-Families.* New York: Bantam Books, 1982.

————.*The Boys and Girls Book About Divorce.* New York: Bantam Books, 1971.

Grollman, Earl A. (ed.). *Explaining Divorce to Children.* Boston: Beacon Press, 1969.

Halpern, Howard M. *Cutting Loose: An Adult Guide to Coming to Terms with Your Parents.* New York: Bantam Books, 1978.

Herman, Judith Lewis. *Father–Daughter Incest.* Cambridge, Mass.: Harvard University Press, 1981.

Irving, Howard. "Single Parenting: An Empirical Analysis Utilizing a Large Data Base." *Family Process*, 1984, 23: 261–569.

Jackson, Michael and Jessica. *Your Father's Not Coming Home Anymore.* New York: Ace Books, 1982.

Krantzler, Mel. *Creative Divorce.* New York: New American Library, 1975.

Legal Remedies for Child Snatching. Summer 1981 issue of *Family Law Quarterly*, Vol. XV, No. 2.

Mead, Margaret. *Male and Female: A Study of the Sexes in a Changing World.* New York: Morrow/Quill Paperbacks, 1967.

McKay, Matthew, Peter D. Rogers, Joan Blades, and Richard Gosse. *The Divorce Book.* Oakland, Calif.: New Harbinger Publications, 1984.

Mitchell, Juliet. *Women: The Longest Revolution.* New York: Pantheon Books, 1984.

Morawetz, Anita. "The Single-Parent Family: An Author's Reflection." *Family Process,* 1984, 23:571–576.

Olshaker, Bennett. *What Shall We Tell the Kids?* New York: Arbor House, 1971.

Renvoize, Jean. *Incest: A Family Pattern.* London: Routledge & Kegan Paul, 1981.

Rofes, Eric. (ed.). *The Kids' Book of Divorce.* New York: Vintage Books, 1982.

Rothman, Sheila M. *Woman's Proper Place.* New York: Basic Books, 1978.

Shorter, Edward. *The Making of the Modern Family.* New York: Basic Books, 1975.

Silver, Gerald A. and Myrna. *Weekend Fathers.* Los Angeles: Stratford Press, 1981.

Smith, Liz. *The Mother Book.* New York: Doubleday, 1978.

Sprouse, Mary L. *Taxable You.* New York: Penguin Books, 1984.

Troyer, Warner. *Divorced Kids.* Toronto: Clarke Irwin, 1979.

Wallerstein, Judith S. and Joan Berlin Kelly. *Surviving the Breakup.* New York: Basic Books, 1980.

Ware, Ciji. *Sharing Parenthood After Divorce.* New York: Bantam Books, 1984.

Warner, Ralph, and Toni Ihara. *California Marriage and Divorce Law,* 6th ed. Berkeley, Calif.: Nolo Press, 1984.

Women in Transition Inc., *A Feminist Handbook on Separation and Divorce.* New York: Charles Scribner's, 1975.

OTHER REFERENCES

Federal Employees Compensation Act, Committee on Labor and Public Welfare, United States Senate, 1974.

Parental Kidnapping Prevention Act, 96th Congress, 1st Session S. 105, 1979.

Revised Uniform Reciprocal Enforcement of Support Act, National Conference of Commissioners on Uniform State Laws, 1968.

Uniform Marriage and Divorce Act, National Conference of Commissioners on Uniform State Laws, 1970.